GCS
REVISION
RESCUE

HIGHER
MATHS

**Philip Hooper &
Sheila Hunt**

Hodder & Stoughton
A MEMBER OF THE HODDER HEADLINE GROUP

A catalogue record for this title is available from the British Library.

ISBN 0340 775 688

First published 2000
Impression number 10 9 8 7 6 5 4 3 2 1
Year 2005 2004 2003 2002 2001 2000 ·

Editorial, design and production by Hart McLeod, Cambridge

Printed in Spain by Graphycems for Hodder & Stoughton Educational, a division of Hodder Headline Plc
338 Euston Road, London NW1 3BH

Contents

Revision Rescue

The pages that follow contain a gold mine of information on how you can achieve success in your exams. Read them and apply the information, and you will be able to spend less, but more efficient, time studying, with better results.

This section gives you vital information on how to remember more while you are learning and how to remember more after you have finished studying. It explains

- how to use special techniques to improve your memory
- how to use a revolutionary note-taking technique called Mind Mapping that will double your memory and help you to write essays and answer exam questions
- how to read everything faster while at the same time improving your comprehension and concentration

Your amazing memory

There are five important things you must know about your brain and memory to revolutionise your school life.

1 how your memory ('recall') works while you are learning
2 how your memory works after you have finished learning
3 how to use Mind Maps – a special technique for helping you with all aspects of your studies
4 how to increase your reading speed
5 how to zap your revision

1 Recall during learning – the need for breaks

When you are studying, your memory can concentrate, understand and remember well for between 20 and 45 minutes at a time. Then it needs a break. If you carry on for longer than this without one, your memory starts to break down! If you study for hours non-stop, you will remember only a fraction of what you have been trying to learn, and

you will have wasted valuable revision time.

So, ideally, study for less than an hour, then take a five- to ten-minute break. During the break listen to music, go for a walk, do some exercise, or just daydream. (Daydreaming is a necessary brain-power booster – geniuses do it regularly.) During the break your brain will be sorting out what it has been learning, and you will go back to your books with the new information safely stored and organised in your memory banks.

2 Recall after learning – the waves of your memory

What do you think begins to happen to your memory straight after you have finished learning something? Does it immediately start forgetting? No! Your brain actually increases its power and carries on remembering. For a short time after your study session, your brain integrates the information, making a more complete picture of everything it has just learnt. Only then does the rapid decline in memory begin, and as much as 80 per cent of what you have learnt can be forgotten in a day.

However, if you catch the top of the wave of your memory, and briefly review (look back over) what you have been revising at the correct time, the memory is stamped in far more strongly, and stays at the crest of the wave for a much longer time. To maximise your brain's power to remember, take a few minutes and use a Mind Map to review what you have learnt at the end of a day. Then review it at the end of a week, again at the end of the month, and finally a week before the exams. That way you'll ride your memory wave all the way to your exam – and beyond!

Amazing as your memory is (think of everything you actually have stored in your brain at this moment) the principles on which it operates are very simple. Your brain will remember if it:

(a) has an image (a picture or a symbol);

(b) has that image fixed

(c) can link that image to something else.

3 The Mind Map® – a picture of the way you think

Do you like taking notes? More importantly, do you like having to go back over and learn them before exams? Most students I know certainly do not! And how do you take your notes? Most people take notes on lined paper, using blue or black ink. The result, visually, is boring! And what does your brain do when it is bored? It turns off, tunes out, and goes to sleep! Add a dash of colour, rhythm, imagination, and the whole note-taking process becomes much more fun, uses more of your brain's abilities, and improves your recall and understanding.

A Mind Map mirrors the way your brain works. It can be used for note-taking from books or in class, for reviewing what you have just studied, for revising, and for essay planning for coursework and in exams. It uses all your memory's natural techniques to build up your rapidly growing 'memory muscle'.

You will find sample Mind Maps at the end of this book. Study them, add some colour, personalise them, and then have a go at drawing your own – you'll remember them far better! Put them on your walls and in your files for a quick-and-easy review of the topic.

How to draw a Mind Map®

1 Start in the middle of the page with the page turned sideways. This gives your brain the maximum room for its thoughts.

2 Always start by drawing a small picture or symbol. Why? Because a picture is worth a thousand words to your brain. And try to use at least three colours, as colour helps your memory even more.

3 Let your thoughts flow, and write or draw your ideas on coloured branching lines connected to your central image. These key symbols and words are the headings for your topic.

4 Then add facts and ideas by drawing more, smaller, branches on to the appropriate main branches, just like a tree.

5 Always print your word clearly on its line. Use only one word per line.

6 To link ideas and on different branches, use arrows, colours, underlining and boxes.

How to read a Mind Map®

1 Begin in the centre, the focus of your topic.

2 The words/images attached to the centre are like chapter headings, so read them next.

3 Always read out from the centre, in every direction (even on the left-hand side, where you will have to read from right to left, instead of the usual left to right).

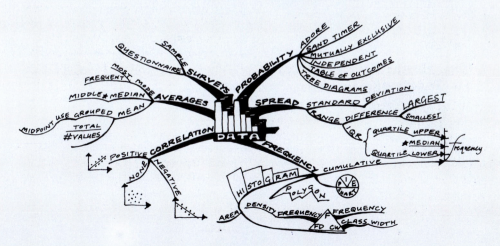

4 Super speed reading

It seems incredible, but it's been proved – the faster you read, the more you understand and remember! So here are some tips to help you to practise reading faster – you'll cover the ground more quickly, remember more, and have more time for revision!

First read the whole text (whether it's a lengthy book or an exam paper) very quickly, to give your brain an overall idea of what's ahead and get it working. (It's like sending out a scout to look at the territory you have to cover – it's much easier when you know what to expect!) Then read the text again for more detailed information.

Have the text a reasonable distance away from your eyes. In this way your eye/brain system will be able to see more at a glance, and will naturally begin to read faster.

Take in groups of words at a time. Rather than reading 'slowly and carefully' read faster, more enthusiastically. Your comprehension will rocket!

Take in phrases rather than single words while you read.

Use a guide. Your eyes are designed to follow movement, so a thin pencil underneath the lines you are reading, moved smoothly along, will 'pull' your eyes to faster speeds.

5 And finally...

Have fun while you learn – studies show that those people who enjoy what they are doing understand and remember it more, and generally do it better.

Use your teachers as resource centres. Ask them for help with specific topics and with more general advice on how you can improve your all-round performance.

Personalise your Revision Rescue by underlining and highlighting, by adding notes and pictures. Allow your brain to have a conversation with it!

Tony Buzan

How to use this book

Revision Rescue: Mathematics – Higher Level is clearly divided into subject chapters and topic sections. Each contains the facts you need to know, with key words highlighted for extra clarity.

The tinted boxes contain useful tips and hints, words and ideas to remember and short quizzes to test your knowledge and highlight areas that you may need to revise again.

Each chapter ends with a longer quiz related to the topic covered.

The Exam Emergency Service on Teletext

As you revise, you can boost your knowledge even further with a free exam emergency service on Teletext.

At key revision times, this service offers subject-specific advice, tips and hints for effective exam performance and guidance for planning you revision... until the very last minute! You will find a wide range of subject quizzes, which change regularly so you can test your knowledge again and again.

Last minute cramming? The most important topics in this section are: Indices; Rational and irrational numbers; Upper and lower bounds.

Indices

Addition and division with indices

For multiplication use **TIP**: **T**imes **I**ndices **P**lus –

$x^2 \times x^5 = x^7$.

For division use **DIM**: **D**ivide **I**ndices **M**inus –

$\dfrac{x^9}{x^4} = x^5$.

For powers of variables with indices, use **PIT**: **P**ower **I**ndices **T**imes –

$$(x^2)^3 = x^6 \qquad \sqrt[3]{(x^7)} = (x^7)^{1/3} = x^{7/3}.$$

Fractional indices

$$x^{1/2} = \sqrt{x} \qquad x^{1/3} = \sqrt[3]{x}.$$

Negative indices

$$x^{-1} = \dfrac{1}{x} \qquad x^{-2} = \dfrac{1}{x^2} \qquad 2x^{-3} = \dfrac{2}{x^3}.$$

Indices of zero

Any number to the power of zero equals 1:
e.g. $10^0 = 1$ $\qquad x^0 = 1$.

Question

Write $\dfrac{\sqrt{x}}{yz^3}$ in the form $x^p y^q z^r$.

Answer

$x^{\frac{1}{2}} y^{-1} z^{-3}$.

Question

Evaluate $(1.2 \times 10^{200}) \div (4.0 \times 10^{145})$

Write your answer in standard index form.

Answer

$$\frac{1.2 \times 10^{200}}{4.0 \times 10^{145}} = 0.3 \times 10^{55}$$

because $1.2 \div 4 = 0.3$
and using DIM, $200 - 145 = 55$

$$= 0.3 \times 10 \times 10^{54}$$
$$= 3 \times 10^{54}.$$

Questions

Simplify: **(i)** $x^{-2}x^3\sqrt{x}$ **(ii)** $\sqrt{x^2 y^6}$.

Answers

(i) Using TIP, $x^{-2}x^3\sqrt{x} = x^{-2+3+0.5} = x^{1.5}$

(ii) Using PIT, $\sqrt{x^2 y^6} = (x^2 y^6)^{0.5} = xy^3$.

Note that this does not work for the power of a sum:

$\sqrt{x^2 + y^2}$ is not $x + y$, and $(x + y)^2$ is not $x^2 + y^2$.

Question

Find k if $\sqrt{8} = 4^k$.

Answer

Express both sides as powers of 2
$$\sqrt{8} = 4^k$$
$$(2^3)^{0.5} = (2^2)^k$$
$$2^{1.5} = 2^{2k}$$
Equate powers
$$1.5 = 2k$$
$$k = 0.75.$$

Question

Simplify $\sqrt{63} + \sqrt{28}$.

Answer

Factorise squared numbers out of each number
$$\sqrt{63} + \sqrt{28} = \sqrt{9} \times \sqrt{7} + \sqrt{4} \times \sqrt{7}$$
$$= 3\sqrt{7} + 2\sqrt{7} = 5\sqrt{7}.$$

Standard form

Example

When using your calculator, learn how to use the $\boxed{\text{EXP}}$ or $\boxed{\text{EE}}$ key.
3×10^8 should be entered as 3 $\boxed{\text{EXP}}$ 8 (or 3 $\boxed{\text{EE}}$ 8), not 3×10 $\boxed{\text{EXP}}$ 8.

Questions

The speed of light is approximately 300 000 000 m/s.

(a) Write 300 000 000 in standard form.

(b) How far does light travel in 1 year?

Give your answer in metres in standard index form.

(c) How long does it take light to travel 1 metre?

Give your answer in seconds in standard index form.

Answers

(a) 3×10^8.

(b) Number of seconds in a year = $60 \times 60 \times 24 \times 365$
$$= 31\ 536\ 000.$$
In a year, light travels $3 \times 10^8 \times 31\ 536\ 000 = 9.46 \times 10^{15}$ metres.

(c) Time = $\dfrac{\text{Distance}}{\text{Speed}} = \dfrac{1}{3 \times 10^8} = 3.3 \times 10^{-9}$ seconds.

Question

What is the product of 3.5×10^{120} and 7.2×10^{108}?
Give your answer in standard index form.

Answer

These numbers are too large for most calculators.

$(3.5 \times 10^{120}) \times (7.2 \times 10^{108}) = 25.2 \times 10^{228}$ using TIP.

Converting to standard form: $25.2 \times 10^{228} = 2.52 \times 10 \times 10^{228}$
$$= 2.52 \times 10^{229}.$$

Calculations involving upper and lower bounds

Questions

Write as an interval approximation (or 'Write down the lower and upper bounds of the following'):

(i) 0.41 to 2 d.p.

(ii) 10 m to the nearest metre.

(iii) 60 000 to the nearest 10 000.

Answers

(i) 0.405, 0.415.

(ii) 9.5 m, 10.5 m.

(iii) 55 000, 65 000.

Question

The area of a rectangle is 550 cm^2 to 2 s.f.
If the height of the rectangle is 16 cm to the nearest whole number, find the maximum and minimum possible widths of the rectangle.
Give your answers to 1 d.p.

Answer

The upper and lower bounds of the area of the rectangle are 555 cm^2 and 545 cm^2, and of the height are 16.5 cm and 15.5 cm. When dividing two numbers, the maximum result is the bigger numerator divided by the smaller denominator:

$$\text{Maximum width} = \frac{\text{maximum area}}{\text{minimum height}}$$

$$= \frac{555}{15.5} = 35.8 \text{ cm.}$$

The opposite is true for the minimum:

$$\text{Minimum width} = \frac{\text{minimum area}}{\text{maximum height}}$$

$$= \frac{545}{16.5} = 33.0 \text{ cm.}$$

Rational and irrational numbers

Rational numbers are numbers which may be expressed in the form $\frac{a}{b}$ where a and b are integers (whole numbers).
The main types of rational numbers are:

- **integers** (whole numbers)
- **fractions**
- **finite** (or **terminating**) decimals
- **recurring** decimals.

The main types of **irrational numbers** you will encounter are π and the square roots of non-square numbers, e.g. $\sqrt{2}$, $\sqrt{3}$, $\sqrt{5}$, $\sqrt{6}$, $\sqrt{7}$, etc.

Question

Find an irrational number between 4 and 5.

Answer

Since $4^2 = 16$ and $5^2 = 25$, the answer may be the square root of any number between 16 and 25 exclusive, i.e. $\sqrt{17}$, $\sqrt{18}$, ..., $\sqrt{24}$.

Note

Do not write your answer as a random set of figures with dots at the end, such as 4.245617058.... This will not get any marks.

Questions

(a) Find a number x other than 2 such that $\sqrt{2} \times \sqrt{x}$ is a rational number.

(b) Find a number y such that $\pi + y$ is a rational number.

Answers

(a) Take any number other than 2 that is divisible by 2.
The example below uses 10.
$$\sqrt{2} \times \sqrt{x} = 10$$
$$\sqrt{2x} = 10$$
$$2x = 100$$
$$x = 50.$$
or, taking 4: $2x = 16 \Rightarrow x = 8$.

(b) y must be a number consisting of two parts: a rational part and a part which cancels out with π, e.g. $y = 4 - \pi$.

Recurring decimals

The 999 rule

Example

$$0.44444... = \frac{4}{9}$$

$$0.23232323... = \frac{23}{99}$$

$$0.142142142... = \frac{142}{999}.$$

The conventional method

Questions

Express (**a**) 0.47474747... and (**b**) 0.127777... in the form $\frac{a}{b}$ where a and b are integers.

Answers

The aim is to find two numbers with the same recurring decimal after the decimal point.

(**a**)   Let $x = 0.47474747...$ (1)

       $100x = 47.474747...$ (2)

       $99x = 47$ (2) – (1)

$$x = \frac{47}{99}$$

(**b**)   Let $x = 0.127777...$

       $100x = 12.7777...$ (1)

       $1000x = 127.7777...$ (2)

       $900x = 115$ (2) – (1)

$$x = \frac{115}{900} = \frac{23}{180}.$$

Direct and inverse proportion

Direct proportion

'**Is proportional to**' may be written as '**varies directly with**' or '**is directly proportional to**'.

In the examples below, k is a constant.

Examples

y is proportional to $x \Rightarrow y \propto x \Rightarrow y = kx$.
y is proportional to the square of $x \Rightarrow y \propto x^2 \Rightarrow y = kx^2$.

Inverse proportion

'**Is inversely proportional to**' may also be written as '**varies indirectly with**'.

Example

y is inversely proportional to the square root of x

$$\Rightarrow y \propto \frac{1}{\sqrt{x}} \Rightarrow y = k \times \frac{1}{\sqrt{x}} \Rightarrow y = \frac{k}{\sqrt{x}}.$$

With both direct and inverse proportion, you may replace the '$\propto$' sign with '$= k \times$'.

Questions

y is proportional to the square root of x.
If $y = 7.7$ when $x = 17.9$, find:

(**a**) y when $x = 22.9$

(**b**) x when $y = 10.2$

Give your answers to 1 d.p.

Answers

y is proportional to the square root of $x \Rightarrow y \propto \sqrt{x} \Rightarrow y = k\sqrt{x}$.
Now find k using the initial values of x and y:

$7.7 = k\sqrt{17.9} \Rightarrow k = 1.820$.

(**a**) $y = 1.820 \times \sqrt{22.9} = 8.7$

(**b**) $x = (10.2 \div 1.820)^2 = 31.4$.

Exponential growth and decay

Remember

AP^T: amount $\times$ percentage^{time}.

Question

A population is predicted to grow at the rate of 5% per year. If it is currently 2.2 million people, what would you expect it to be in 6 years time?

Answer

Write 5% as $1 + 0.05 = 1.05$ – this is the multiplier to find the following year's population. As there are 6 years, we must put this multiplier to the power of six: **using AP^T** (where **A** = Initial amount, **P** = Percentage and **T** = Time),

expected population after 6 years = 2.2×1.05^6

$$= 2.95 \text{ million people.}$$

Question

A car is depreciating in value by 8% per year. If it is currently valued at £21 000, what would you expect it to be worth in 9 years time?

Answer

As the car is losing value, write the percentage as $1 - 0.08 = 0.92$.

Using AP^T, predicted value after 9 years = $21\,000 \times 0.92^9$

$$= £9\,915 \text{ to the nearest pound.}$$

Revision recap

A Brain-teaser on indices

Questions

(a) Find k if $\sqrt{27} = 3^k$.

(b) A cuboid has sides of length $\sqrt{27}$, 9 and 81 cm. If its volume in cubic centimetres is 3^y, find y.

Answers

(a) $(3^3)^{0.5} = 3^{1.5}$ $k = 1.5$.

(b) If written in the form 3^y, the indices of $\sqrt{27}$, 9 and 81 are 1.5, 2 and 4 respectively. Using TIP, $y = 1.5 + 2 + 4 = 7.5$.

In a rush? The most likely topics to come up from this section are: Simultaneous equations; Quadratic expressions and equations; Simultaneous equations from practical situations.

Simultaneous equations

In the expression $7x^2 - 6y$, the coefficient of x^2 is 7 and the coefficient of y is –6.

Method for solving by elimination

(1) Firstly make the coefficients (ignoring signs) of either the x- or the y-terms the same by multiplying one or both equations.

(2) Box the terms which you intend to cancel out. If the signs of the variables are the **same**, **take** one equation from the other; if the signs of the variables are **opposite**, **plus** the two equations (remember **STOP**: **s**ame **t**ake, **o**pposite **p**lus).

(3) This gives an equation in one variable alone. Solve this.

(4) Substitute the value you found in (3) into one of the original equations, to find the other variable.

(5) Check your values of x and y in the other equation.

Question

Solve the simultaneous equations:
$$4x - 5y = 17$$
$$3x + 2y = 30$$

Answer

(1) To make the coefficients of y the same (ignoring signs), multiply the first equation by 2 and the second by 5 (alternatively, you could multiply them by 3 and 4 respectively to make the coefficients of the x-terms the same).
$$8x - 10y = 34$$
$$15x + 10y = 150$$

(2) Box the y-terms. As the y-terms have **o**pposite signs, **STOP** says to **p**lus the two equations.

$$8x \boxed{- 10y} = 34$$
$$15x \boxed{+ 10y} = 150 \quad +$$

(3) $\quad\quad 23x \quad\quad\; = 184$

$\quad\quad\quad\; x \quad\quad\; = 8$

(4) Using $3x + 2y = 30$, $24 + 2y = 30$, so $y = 3$.

(5) Checking using $4x - 5y = 17$, $32 - 15 = 17$ ✓ .

Method for solving by substitution

Use this method when one of the equations is given in the form '$x =$' or '$y =$'.
Substitute for x or y in the other equation, **remembering to put the substituted expression in brackets.** Solve, substitute your answer into one of the original equations to find the other variable, then check.

Question

Solve the simultaneous equations. $3x - y = 5$
$$y = 2x - 1$$

Answer

Replace the y in the first equation with $(2x - 1)$.
$3x - (2x - 1) = 5 \Rightarrow 3x - 2x + 1 = 5 \Rightarrow x + 1 = 5 \Rightarrow x = 4$.
Substituting into $y = 2x - 1$ gives $y = 2 \times 4 - 1 = 7$.
Checking in $3x - y = 5$ gives $3 \times 4 - 7 = 5$ ✓ So $x = 4$, $y = 7$.

Inequalities

Linear inequalities

The method for solving linear inequalities is similar to that of linear equations, except for two rules:

Rule 1: Change sides, change signs. For example, if $5 > 2$, then $2 < 5$.
Rule 2: If you multiply or divide both sides by a negative number, the inequality reverses. For example, multiplying both sides of $6 \geqslant -3$ through by -1 gives $-6 \leqslant 3$. Rule 1 is much easier to use than Rule 2, so if the term in x is negative, take it over to the other side.

Example

Find the range of values of x for which $7 - 2x > 1$
x is negative, take it over to the other side: $7 > 2x + 1$
$$6 > 2x$$
$$3 > x \qquad \textbf{Using rule 1:} \qquad x < 3.$$

Quadratic inequalites

These are not as easy as they look: you cannot simply square root both sides.
For $x^2 \leqslant a^2$, use B $\leqslant$ TW $\leqslant\leqslant$ N $-a$ and a, or $-a \leqslant x \leqslant a$.
For $x^2 > a^2$, use <>UTSII>E $-a$ and a, $x < -a$, i.e. $x > a$.

Questions

Find the range of values of x which satisfy the inequalities:
(**a**) $x^2 < 4$ (**b**) $x^2 \geqslant 25$.

Answers

(**a**) $-2 < x < 2$ (**b**) $x \leqslant -5$, $x \geqslant 5$.

Formula rearrangement

If the variable that you need to make the subject of the formula:

- has a negative coefficient or is on the denominator, take it to the other side
- appears in two different terms, then take both of these terms to one side of the equation, all other terms to the other side, then factorise and divide
- is multiplied by a fraction, then treat the fraction as the numerator divided by the denominator and take one of these over at a time.

Questions

Make x the subject of the following formulae:

(i) $e = f - x$

(ii) $v = \dfrac{u}{x}$

(iii) $m = \dfrac{n}{l - x}$

(iv) $sx = tx + r$

(v) $b - ax = cx + ad$

(vi) $V = \dfrac{1}{4}\pi x^2 h$

(vii) $a = \sqrt[3]{b - x^2}$.

Answers

(i) The coefficient of x is negative, so take it over: a positive coefficient is much easier to work with.

$e + x = f \Rightarrow x = f - e$

(ii) If x is in the denominator, you should take it over first:

$vx = u \Rightarrow x = \dfrac{u}{v}$

(iii) Take the denominator over first, then either expand out or divide both sides by m:

$m(l - x) = n \Rightarrow ml - mx = n \Rightarrow ml - n = mx$

$\Rightarrow x = \dfrac{ml - n}{m}$

or $\Rightarrow l - x = \dfrac{n}{m} \Rightarrow l = \dfrac{n}{m} + x \Rightarrow x = l - \dfrac{n}{m}$

The answers may look different but they are different ways of writing the same formula.

(iv) When the x appears in two different terms, take the terms containing this variable to one side of the equation and all other terms to the other side, then factorise:

$$sx - tx = r \Rightarrow x(s - t) = r \Rightarrow x = \frac{r}{s - t}$$

(v) To minimise the number of negative terms, take the terms in x on to the right-hand side, and the others over to the left-hand side, then factorise and divide:

$$b - ad = cx + ax \Rightarrow b - ad = x(c + a) \Rightarrow x = \frac{b - ad}{c + a}$$

(vi) Treat the $\frac{1}{4}$ as $1 \div 4$, then take πh (the coefficient of x^2) over, then square root:

$$V = \frac{\pi x^2 h}{4} \Rightarrow x^2 = \frac{4V}{\pi h} \Rightarrow x = \pm \sqrt{\frac{4V}{\pi h}}$$

Strictly, when square rooting, a $\pm$ should be put in front of the root sign.

(vii) $a^3 = b - x^2 \Rightarrow x^2 = b - a^3 \Rightarrow x = \pm\sqrt{b - a^3}$.

Single bracket factorisation

Example

Factorise $x^2 - 2x$.
Look for common factors of x^2 and $-2x$. As x goes into both terms, write it outside the single bracket:
$x($
Either work out what multiplies with x to give x^2 and $-2x$:
$x \times x = x^2$ and $x \times -2 = -2x$
or divide each term through by x to leave $x - 2$:
so $x^2 - 2x = x(x - 2)$.

Example

Factorise $4p^2q + 2pq^2$
As 2, p and q go into both terms, write $2pq$ outside the bracket:
$2pq($
Either find what $2pq$ multiples with to give $4p^2q$ and $+ 2pq^2$:
$2pq \times 2p = 4p^2q$ and $2pq \times q = +2pq^2$
or divide each term through by 2, p and q to leave $2p + q$
$4p^2q + 2pq^2 = 2pq(2p + q)$.

Note

Check that the expansion of your factorised expression is the same as the one in the question.

Quadratic expressions and equations

Expanding quadratics

Use **FOIL**: **F**irst, **O**uter, **I**nner, **L**ast.

Example

Expand $(2x - 3)(x + 7)$.

$$\quad\quad\quad\quad\quad\quad \textbf{First O}uter \textbf{I}nner \textbf{L}ast$$
$$(2x - 3)(x + 7) = 2x^2 + 14x - 3x - 21$$
$$= 2x^2 + 11x - 21.$$

Factorising quadratics with an x^2 coefficient of 1

Type 1: the constant term is positive, so factors have the same sign.
Type 1a: the x-term is positive, so both terms are positive.

Example

Factorise $x^2 + 7x + 12$.

List all the pairs of factors of the constant term. The correct pair sums to the coefficient of the x-term.

$x^2 + 7x + 12$	+12	+6	+4
	+1	+2	+3
	+13	+8	+7

$= (x + 4)(x + 3)$.

Type 1: the constant term is positive, so factors have the same sign.
Type 1b: the x-term is negative, so both terms are negative.

Example

Factorise $x^2 - 14x + 40$	−40	−20	−10	−8
	−1	−2	−4	−5
	−41	−22	−14	−13

$= (x - 10)(x - 4)$.

Type 2: the constant term is negative, so the signs are different.
Type 2a: the x-term is positive, so the larger factor is positive.

Example

Factorise $x^2 + 4x - 45$	+45	+15	+9
	−1	−3	−5
	+44	+12	+4

$= (x + 9)(x - 5)$.

Type 2: the constant term is negative, so the signs are different.
Type 2b: the x-term is negative, so the larger factor is negative.

Example

Factorise $x^2 - 7x - 60$

-60	-30	-20	-15	-12	-10
$+1$	$+2$	$+3$	$+4$	$+5$	$+6$
-59	-28	-17	-11	-7	-4

$= (x - 12)(x + 5)$.

Difference of two squares

i.e. two squared terms, separated by a minus sign.

Questions

Factorise: **(i)** $x^2 - 16$ **(ii)** $a^2 - b^2$ **(iii)** $2x^2 - 50$.

Answers

(i) $x^2 - 16 = (x - 4)(x + 4)$

(ii) $a^2 - b^2 = (a - b)(a + b)$

(iii) $2x^2 - 50 = 2(x^2 - 25) = 2(x - 5)(x + 5)$.

Factorising quadratic expressions when the coefficient of x^2 is not 1

This is usually done by trial and error. It is easier if the coefficient of x^2 is a prime number: then there is only one way in which it can be factorised.

Questions

Factorise: **(i)** $5x^2 - 23x + 12$ **(ii)** $2x^2 + x - 10$.

Answers

(i) Start by factorising the x-term: $(5x \quad)(x \quad)$
The constant, $+12$, has 3 different pairs of factors: 12, 1 or 6, 2 or 4, 3.
Using trial and error gives $(5x - 3)(x - 4)$

(ii) $2x^2 + x - 10 = (2x + 5)(x - 2)$.

Solving quadratics by factorisation

Factorising a quadratic equation gives the product of two expressions equating to zero. If the product of two numbers is zero, one of the two numbers must be zero. Similarly for two expressions:
if $(2x - 1)(x + 3) = 0$ then either $\quad 2x - 1 = 0$ or $x + 3 = 0$

so $\quad x = \frac{1}{2}$ or $x = -3$.

20

Question

Find the values of x for which $3x^2 - 14x + 15 = 0$.

Answer

$(3x - 5)(x - 3) = 0$

$3x - 5 = 0$ or $x - 3 = 0$

$x = 1\frac{2}{3}$ or $x = 3$.

Factorising in pairs

This is an alternative method of factorising quadratics. To factorise $ax^2 + bx + c$, find two numbers which have a product of ac and a sum of b, split the term in x up into two terms using these two numbers as coefficients, and factorise in two pairs, then factorise again.

Examples

(**a**) Factorise $6x^2 + 7x - 20$

(**b**) Solve $6x^2 + 7x - 20 = 0$

Solution

(**a**) $ac = -120$ $b = 7$

15 and -8 have a product of -120 and a sum of 7, so split up $7x$ into $15x - 8x$ (or $-8x + 15x$):

$6x^2 + 7x - 20 = 6x^2 + 15x - 8x - 20$

then factorise in pairs, ensuring that the expressions in the brackets are the same:

$= 3x(2x + 5) - 4(2x + 5)$

next factorise out the expression in the brackets:

$= (2x + 5)(3x - 4)$

[If you cannot see how this line has been found from the previous line, substitute $y = 2x + 5$ to give $3xy - 4y$ which factorises to $y(3x - 4) = (2x + 5)(3x - 4)$]

(**b**) $(2x + 5)(3x - 4) = 0$

Equate each of the two expressions inside the brackets to zero:

$2x + 5 = 0$ $3x - 4 = 0$

$x = \frac{-5}{2}$ $x = \frac{4}{3}$

This method can also be used for the type of expression overleaf.

Example

Factorise $pq - p + q^2 - q$

Solution

Factorise $pq - p$ and $+ q^2 - q$ separately. Factorise each of the two expressions, making the term inside each pair of brackets the same.

$$pq - p + q^2 - q = p(q - 1) + q(q - 1) = (q - 1)(p + q)$$

Question

Factorise $x^2 - 2x - xy + 2y$.

Answer

Factorising the first pair of terms gives $x^2 - 2x = x(x - 2)$. Factorise the second pair of terms, making sure that $(x - 2)$ is left inside the brackets: $-xy + 2y = -y(x - 2)$

$$x^2 - 2x - xy + 2y = x(x - 2) - y(x - 2)$$
$$= (x - 2)(x - y).$$

Quadratic formula

The formula for the solution of the general quadratic $ax^2 + bx + c = 0$

is $x = \dfrac{-b \pm \sqrt{b^2 - 4ac}}{2a}$.

Make sure that equations are in the form $ax^2 + bx + c = 0$ before using the formula, e.g.

$$3x^2 - 2x = 2 \Rightarrow 3x^2 - 2x - 2 = 0$$

$$7 + \frac{3}{x} = 2x \Rightarrow 7x + 3 = 2x^2 \Rightarrow 2x^2 - 7x - 3 = 0.$$

Question

Solve $5x^2 + 6x - 10 = 0$ to 2 d.p.

Answer

$a = 5$, $b = 6$ and $c = -10$

$$x = \frac{-6 \pm \sqrt{(6)^2 - 4(5)(-10)}}{2(5)}$$

Firstly simplify the expressions inside the square root and the denominator:

$$x = \frac{-6 \pm \sqrt{236}}{10}$$

Calculate the numerator then divide by the denominator: $x = 0.94, -2.14$.

Algebraic fractions

Consider the principles of addition and subtraction of fractions,

e.g. $\dfrac{2}{3} - \dfrac{1}{4}$.

The lowest common denominator (LCD) of 3 and 4 is 12:

$$\dfrac{2}{3} \times \dfrac{4}{4} = \dfrac{8}{12} \quad \dfrac{1}{4} \times \dfrac{3}{3} = \dfrac{3}{12} \text{ so } \dfrac{2}{3} - \dfrac{1}{4} = \dfrac{8-3}{12} = \dfrac{5}{12}.$$

Question

Simplify $\dfrac{3}{x-4} - \dfrac{1}{x-1}$.

Answer

The LCD is $(x-4)(x-1)$

$$\dfrac{3}{x-4} - \dfrac{1}{x-1} = \dfrac{3(x-1)}{(x-4)(x-1)} - \dfrac{(x-4)}{(x-4)(x-1)}$$

Don't forget the brackets around the $(x-4)$

$$= \dfrac{3(x-1)-(x-4)}{(x-4)(x-1)} = \dfrac{3x-3-x+4}{(x-4)(x-1)} = \dfrac{2x+1}{(x-4)(x-1)}.$$

Simplification of algebraic fractions by division

Question

Simplify $\dfrac{x^2-9}{x^2-4x+3}$.

Answer

$$\dfrac{x^2-9}{x^2-4x+3} = \dfrac{(x-3)(x+3)}{(x-3)(x-1)} = \dfrac{x+3}{x-1}.$$

Only cross out terms in the numerator and denominator when the terms are multiplied,

e.g. $\dfrac{x^2-9}{x^2-4x+3}$ is not equal to $\dfrac{-9}{-4x+3}$.

Iteration

Iteration is a method of finding solutions to an equation. It involves repeatedly substituting numbers into a formula, until the outcome is the same as the substituted number. This number is a solution to the given equation.

Questions

(a) Show that $x_{n+1} = \sqrt[3]{x_n^2 + 6}$ is a solution to the equation $x^3 - x^2 - 6 = 0$.

(b) Using this iteration starting with $x_1 = 2.1$, find a solution to the equation $x^3 - x^2 - 6 = 0$ to 2 d.p.

Answers

(a) This question asks you to rearrange $x^3 - x^2 - 6 = 0$ into $x_{n+1} = \sqrt[3]{x_n^2 + 6}$, or vice versa. Start by removing the n and the $n + 1$:

$$x = \sqrt[3]{x^2 + 6} \Rightarrow x^3 = x^2 + 6 \Rightarrow x^3 - x^2 - 6 = 0.$$

(b) $x_2 = \sqrt[3]{x_1^2 + 6} = \sqrt[3]{2.1^2 + 6} = 2.1835$

$x_3 = \sqrt[3]{x_2^2 + 6} = \sqrt[3]{2.1835^2 + 6} = 2.2082$

$x_4 = \sqrt[3]{x_3^2 + 6} = \sqrt[3]{2.2082^2 + 6} = 2.2156$ etc.

The iteration stops changing when $x = 2.22$ to 2 d.p.

Iterations **converge** when they go towards a finite number (as in the example above), otherwise they are said to **diverge**.

Quiz on quadratic expressions
Questions
(1) Expand $(3x - 1)(2x + 5)$.
(2) Factorise the following:
   (a) $x^2 - 11x + 30$
   (b) $x^2 + 12x - 45$
   (c) $x^2 - 10x - 56$
   (d) $x^2 + 19x + 48$.
(3) Factorise fully $50x^2 - 32y^2$.

(1) $6x^2 + 15x - 2x - 5 = 6x^2 + 13x - 5$.
(2) (a) $(x - 6)(x - 5)$
    (b) $(x + 15)(x - 3)$
    (c) $(x - 14)(x + 4)$
    (d) $(x + 16)(x + 3)$.
(3) $2(25x^2 - 16y^2) = 2(5x - 4y)(5x + 4y)$.

Answers

Simultaneous equations from practical situations

Question

The diagram shows a rectangular metal grille. It consists of six horizontal bars, each of length x, and two vertical bars. It is made using 72 cm of metal bar, and covers an area of 96 cm^2.

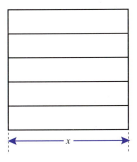

(a) Show that the variable x satisfies the quadratic equation $x^2 - 12x + 32 = 0$.

(b) Solve this equation to find the possible values of the width and height of the grille.

Answer

(a) There is no variable to represent the length of the vertical bar, so call this y. There are six horizontal bars and two vertical bars making a total of 72 cm, so $6x + 2y = 72$. From the given area, $xy = 96$. These are best solved by substitution: make y the subject of the first equation, and substitute this into the second:

$$6x + 2y = 72$$
$$2y = 72 - 6x$$
$$y = 36 - 3x.$$

Substituting into $xy = 96$ gives

$$x(36 - 3x) = 96$$
$$3x^2 - 36x + 96 = 0$$
$$x^2 - 12x + 32 = 0 \text{ by dividing through by 3.}$$

(b)
$$x^2 - 12x + 32 = 0$$
$$(x - 8)(x - 4) = 0$$
$$x - 8 = 0 \text{ or } x - 4 = 0.$$

Therefore $x = 8$ or $x = 4$.

Using $y = 36 - 3x$, when $x = 8$, $y = 12$; when $x = 4$, $y = 24$.

If you could not do the first part of the last question, you may still be able to do part (b). Always look at the later parts of questions even if you can't do the first part.

Questions

A cyclist travels 56 km. She cycles the first 32 km at x km/h and the last 24 km at $(x - 2)$ km/h. The journey takes 8 hours.

(a) Show that the value of x satisfies the equation $x^2 - 9x + 8 = 0$.

(b) Solve this equation to find the value of x.

Answers

(a) You need to set up an equation connecting the time taken on the stages of the trip.

The first 32 km takes $\dfrac{32}{x}$ and the second 24 km takes $\dfrac{24}{x-2}$.

So $\dfrac{32}{x} + \dfrac{24}{x-2} = 8$.

Multiplying both sides through by $x(x - 2)$ gives

$$\frac{32}{x}x(x-2) + \frac{24}{x-2}x(x-2) = 8x(x-2)$$

$$32(x - 2) + 24x = 8x(x - 2)$$

$$32x - 64 + 24x = 8x^2 - 16x$$

$$8x^2 - 72x + 64 = 0$$

$$x^2 - 9x + 8 = 0.$$

(b) $(x - 8)(x - 1) = 0$

$x - 8 = 0$ or $x - 1 = 0$

$x = 8$ or $x = 1$.

However, the solution $x = 1$ would make $(x - 2)$ negative, so the answer is $x = 8$.

Revision recap

Are you okay with exponential growth and decay?

Questions

(1) Bacteria grow at a rate of 5% per minute in a culture. If there were initially 1.1 million cells, how many would you expect there to be after 10 minutes?

(2) A photocopier depreciates by 12% per year. If it cost £16 500 new, what would it be worth at the end of 5 years?

Answers

(1) $1.1 \times 1.05^{10} = 1.79$ million.

(2) $16\,500 \times 0.88^5 = £8\,708$ to the nearest pound.

Sequences

DINO

For sequences with equal differences (linear sequences), use **DINO**.

Questions

For the sequence 5, 8, 11, 14, 17, ... find
(a) the 41st term, and (b) the nth term.

Answers

Do (**b**) before (**a**):

(**b**) Use **DINO**: **DI** is the difference between terms, 3; **N** is n; for **O** put a ring before the first term, and write in it the number that should go before 5 in the sequence, i.e. 2. DINO gives $3n + 2$.

(**a**) Substituting $n = 41$ into $3n + 2$ gives 125.

COSTAS

COSTAS (**C**ube **O**r **S**quare, **T**imes, **A**dd, **S**ubtract) can help to find the nth term of sequences involving n^2 and n^3. To determine whether the sequence involves n^2 or n^3, use the method of differences.

Question

Find the nth term of the sequence
2, 6, 12, 20, 30, ...

Answer

Write down a row of differences, then differences between the differences, etc. until all the numbers in the row are equal:

$$
\begin{array}{ccccccccc}
2 & & 6 & & 12 & & 20 & & 30 \\
& 4 & & 6 & & 8 & & 10 & \\
& & 2 & & 2 & & 2 & &
\end{array}
$$

As the second row of differences are equal, the sequence involves n^2. If it were the third row, it would be a cubic sequence.

n	1	2	3	4	5
n^2	1	4	9	16	25
	2	6	12	20	30

From TAS of COSTAS, the sequence is $n^2 + n$.

Alternative method for finding quadratic or cubic sequences

As the second row of differences are equal, the sequence is quadratic and of the form $an^2 + bn + c$. Substitute when $n = 1$, term = 2; when $n = 2$, term = 6; when $n = 3$, term = 12 into the quadratic and solve using simultaneous equations:

$$
\begin{array}{llll}
n = 3: & 9a + 3b + c = 12 & (3) \\
n = 2: & 4a + 2b + c = 6 & (2) \\
n = 1: & a + b + c = 2 & (1) \\
(3) - (2) & 5a + b = 6 & (4) \\
(2) - (1) & 3a + b = 4 & (5) \\
(4) - (5) & 2a = 2 \\
& a = 1
\end{array}
$$

Substituting into (5) gives $b = 1$
Substituting into (3) gives $c = 0$
So the sequence is $n^2 + n$
If the sequence is cubic, the nth term of the sequence is of the form $an^3 + bn^2 + cn + d$.

OMEN

This method is used to find the nth term of sequences where each term is found by multiplying the previous term by a constant number.

Question

Find the nth term of the sequence
3, 6, 12, 24, ...

Answer

O represents the term that would come before the first i.e. $\frac{3}{2}$.

M is the multiplier, 2.
E means exponent, or 'to the power of'.
N is simply n (as for DINO).
So the nth term is $\frac{3}{2} \times 2^n$.

Triangular sequences

This is the sequence 1, 3, 6, 10, 15, ... and has differences between terms of 2, 3, 4, 5, ... The formula for the nth term is $\frac{1}{2}n(n + 1)$.

Fibonacci sequences

Each term of these sequences is the sum of the previous two terms, 1, 1, 2, 3, 5, 8 ...

Gridlock on graphs? The most important topics are:
Solving equations graphically; Area and tangent to a
curve; Sine, cosine and tangent graphs.

Linear graphs and $y = mx + c$

Most straight-line (linear) graphs can be written in the form $y = mx + c$, where m is
the gradient, and c is the value of the y-intercept.
If y is not the subject of the formula, rearrange the equation before using this
method.

Questions

Write down the gradient and the y-intercept of the following graphs:
(a) $y = 4x - 1$
(b) $y = 1 - x$
(c) $4x + 3y = 24$.

Answers

(a) Gradient = 4, y-intercept = −1
(b) This equation may be rewritten as $y = -x + 1$,
     so the gradient = −1 (the coefficient of x), and the y-intercept = 1

(c) $3y = 24 - 4x \Rightarrow y = 8 - \dfrac{4x}{3}$ Gradient = $-\frac{4}{3}$, y-intercept = 8.

Question

Find the equation of a line which passes through the points (4, 3) and (6, −5).

Answer

Gradient $= \dfrac{\text{change in } y}{\text{change in } x} = \dfrac{-5 - 3}{6 - 4} = -4$

So the equation of the graph is of the form $y = -4x + c$
Substitute either of the pairs of coordinates into this equation to find c:

     using (4, 3): $3 = -4(4) + c$
                     $3 = -16 + c$
                      $c = 19$

So the equation of the line is $y = -4x + 19$

Questions

(a) Find the equation of the line below in the form $y = mx + c$.

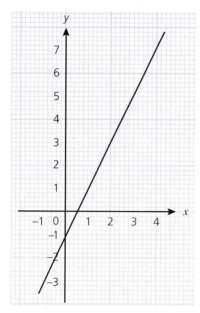

(b) Find an equation of a line parallel to the graph through the point (0,3).

Answers

(a) Using any two points on the line as the hypotenuse of a right-angled triangle, the gradient = 2. The y-intercept is at –1. So the equation of the line is $y = 2x - 1$.

(b) If the new line is parallel, it must have the same gradient. The y-intercept is 3. So an equation of the line is $y = 2x + 3$.

Drawing linear graphs in the form $y = mx + c$

Draw up a table of values, choosing three values of x (usually 0, 1 and 2 are the easiest). Find the corresponding y-values and plot these coordinates on the grid. If they do not lie in a straight line, you have probably made an error in the calculations or plotting the points. Connect the points together, extending the graph to the ends of the grid.

Drawing lines of the form $ax + by = c$

Substitute in the value $x = 0$ to find where the line cuts the y-axis, then $y = 0$ to find where it cuts the x-axis. Plot these on the grid, connect them using a ruler, and extend this line to the ends of the grid. To check, find another point that your line passes through and verify that the x- and y-values satisfy the equation of the line.

Solving equations graphically

In these questions, you are given a graph and asked to solve an equation by drawing an additional line or curve on it. The key is knowing which curve to draw. Take the following steps:

(**1**) Start with the equation you need to solve.

(**2**) Add or subtract to both sides of the equation to make one side the same as the equation of the graph.

(**3**) Draw the graph of $y =$ 'the other side'.

(**4**) Write down the x-values of the points where the two graphs meet.

Questions

The graph of $y = x^3 - x$ is shown below:

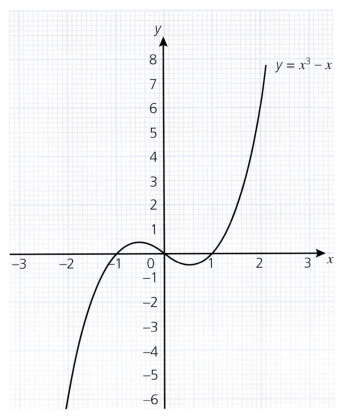

(**a**) Use the graph to find the solution of:
$$x^3 - x = 2.$$

(**b**) By adding a suitable straight line to the grid, use the graph to find the solutions of:
$$x^3 = 2x - 1.$$

Answers

(a) Start with $x^3 - x = 2$.

As one side of the equation is already the same as the equation of the given graph, $y = $ 'the other side' (i.e. $y = 2$) should be drawn on the graph, which gives the solution

$\quad x = 1.5$.

(b) (i) Start with the original equation,

$\quad\quad x^3 = 2x - 1$.

(ii) he equation should be rearranged to have $x^3 - x$ on one side.

$$x^3 = 2x - 1$$

$$\frac{-x \quad\quad -x}{x^3 - x = x - 1}$$

(iii) Therefore $y = x - 1$ should be drawn on the grid to solve the given equation.

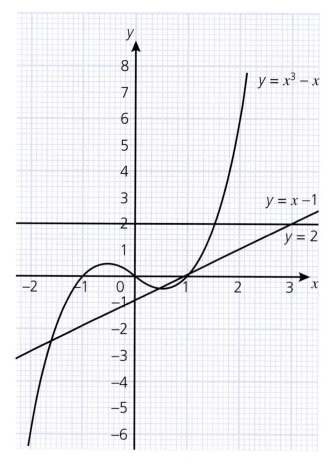

$x = -1.6, 0.4, 1.$

Questions

The diagram below shows the graph of

$$y = x^3 + x^2 - 2x - 3.$$

(a) Use the graph to find the solution to the equation

$$x^3 + x^2 - 2x - 4 = 0.$$

(b) (i) By drawing the graph of $y = x^2$ on the diagram, find the solution of

$$x^3 - 2x - 3 = 0.$$

(ii) Explain why the value of x you have found is the solution to

$$x^3 - 2x - 3 = 0.$$

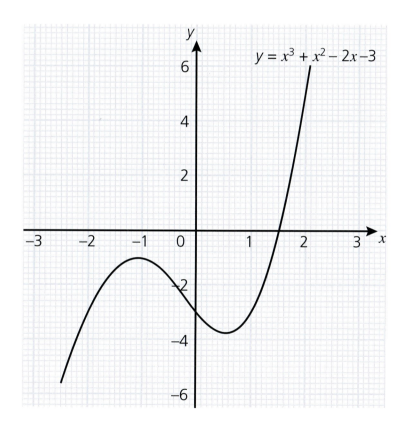

$y = x^3 + x^2 - 2x - 3$

Answers

(a) $x^3 + x^2 - 2x - 4 = 0$

$$\begin{array}{r} +1 \quad +1 \\ \hline x^3 + x^2 - 2x - 3 = 1 \end{array}$$

Therefore, $y = 1$ should be drawn on the diagram, giving the solution
$x = 1.7$.

(b) (i) $x = 1.9$.

(ii) $y = x^3 + x^2 - 2x - 3$ is equated to $y = x^2$.

$$\begin{array}{c} \dfrac{x^3 + x^2 - 2x - 3}{-x^2} = \dfrac{x^2}{-x^2} \\ x^3 \qquad - 2x - 3 = 0 \end{array}$$

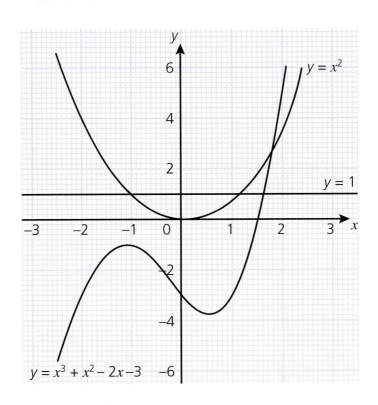

Areas and tangent to a curve

Meanings

The gradient of a curve is 'the vertical axis' **per** 'the horizontal axis'.
For example, on a speed-time graph where the speed is in metres per second and the time is in seconds, the gradient is the metres per second **per** second, or acceleration.
The area under the curve is the same as the product of the units on the horizontal and vertical axes.
For example, on a speed-time graph, the area under the curve is
speed × time = distance.

The trapezium rule

This is a method of finding the approximate area under a graph. Divide the area into a number of vertical strips of equal width. Trapezia are formed by connecting the points where these lines meet the curve.

Area of a trapezium = $\frac{h}{2}(a + b)$.

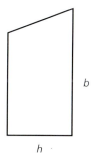

Questions

A bird is travelling in a straight line. Its speed-time graph is shown below.

(**a**) (**i**) Use an appropriate method to find an estimate for the area under the curve.
 (**ii**) What does this area represent?

(**b**) Estimate the acceleration of the bird after 20 seconds.

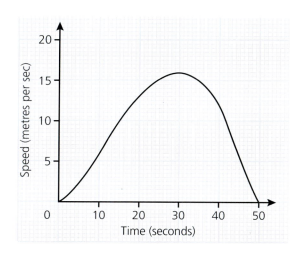

Answers

(**a**) (**i**) Divide the area as shown below:

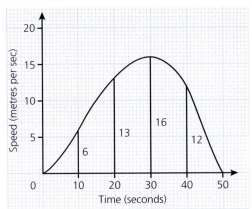

$$\text{Area} \approx \frac{10}{2}(0 + 6) + \frac{10}{2}(6 + 13) + \frac{10}{2}(13 + 16) + \frac{10}{2}(16 + 12) + \frac{10}{2}(12 + 0) = 470.$$

(**ii**) The distance travelled in metres.

(**b**) The acceleration is the gradient of the curve when time = 20 seconds, which is approximately 0.6 m/s².

Question

A car accelerates from rest. Its speed is 8 m/s after 10 seconds, 14 m/s after 20 seconds and 18 m/s after 30 seconds. Find the approximate distance travelled in the first 30 seconds in metres.

Answer

Using the trapezium rule,

$$\text{distance} \approx \frac{10}{2}(0 + 8) + \frac{10}{2}(8 + 14) + \frac{10}{2}(14 + 18)$$
$$= 310 \text{ m}.$$

Revision recap

Touch up your formula rearranging

Question

Make x the subject of the formula $ax + b = cx + d$

Answer

As x appears twice, take all x terms to one side of the equation and all terms without x to the other side: $ax - cx = d - b$

Factorise the left hand side: $x(a - c) = d - b$

Then rearrange to make x the subject:

$$x = \frac{d - b}{a - c}$$

Functions

Adding, subtracting, multiplying or dividing inside the brackets changes $f(x)$ horizontally in the opposite way to what you would expect:
$y = f(x + c)$ moves $f(x)$ to the **left** by c units,
$y = f(x - c)$ moves $f(x)$ to the **right** by c units.

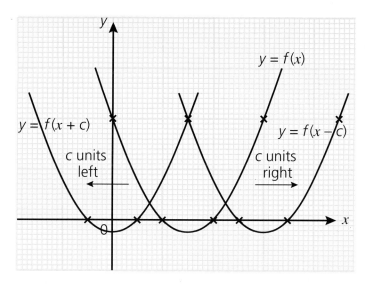

$y = f(2x)$ **squashes** $f(x)$ horizontally by a factor of 2 towards the y-axis.

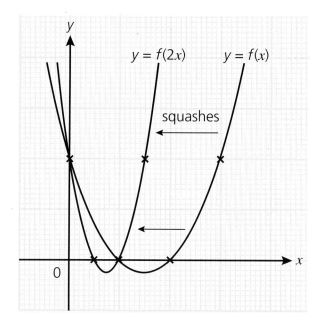

$y = f\left(\frac{x}{2}\right)$ or $f\left(\frac{1}{2}x\right)$ **stretches** $f(x)$ horizontally by a factor of 2 from the y-axis.

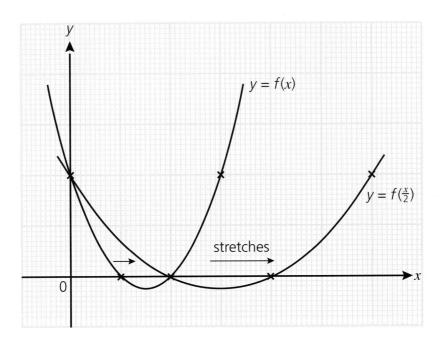

$y = f(-x)$ reflects $f(x)$ in the y-axis.

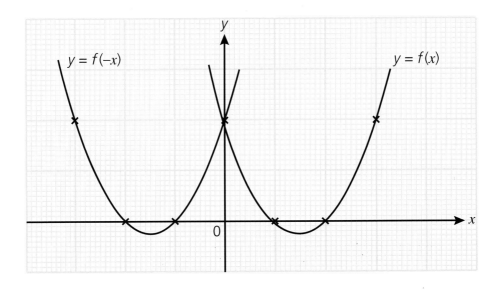

Adding, subtracting, multiplying or dividing outside the $f(x)$ changes $f(x)$ vertically in the way you would expect:

$y = f(x) + c$ moves $f(x)$ **upwards** by c units,

$y = f(x) - c$ moves $f(x)$ **downwards** by c units.

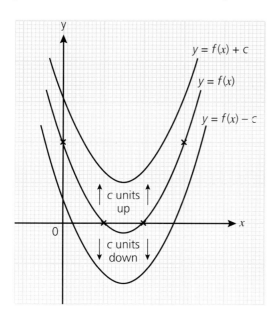

$y = 2f(x)$ **stretches** $f(x)$ vertically by a factor of 2 from the x-axis.

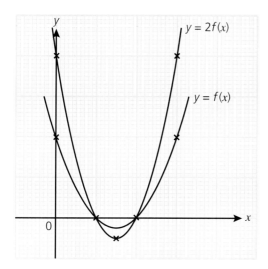

$y = \dfrac{f(x)}{2}$ or $\dfrac{1}{2}f(x)$ **squashes** $f(x)$ vertically by a factor of 2 towards the x-axis.

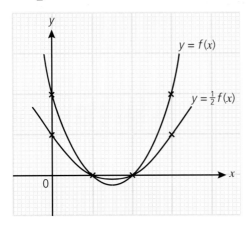

$y = -f(x)$ reflects $f(x)$ in the x-axis.

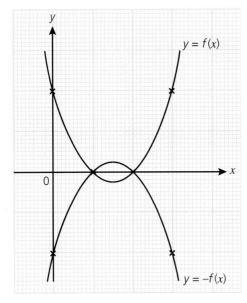

To ensure your sketch of the new graph is accurate, take a number of points on the graph of $f(x)$ (including turning points and points where the graph crosses the axes) and transform them accordingly. Then sketch the graph. Crosses have been shown on the graphs as suggestions of where these points may be placed.

Questions

The graph of $y = x^2$ has been drawn on the grid shown. On the same axes, draw the graphs

(a) $y = (x - 2)^2$ (b) $y = -x^2$.

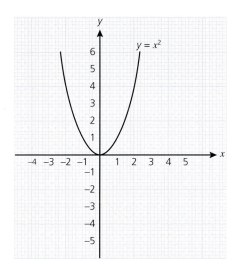

Answers

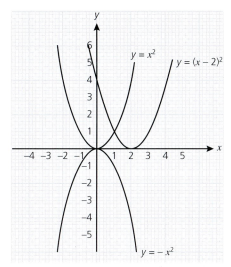

(a) $y = (x - 2)^2$ moves the graph of $y = x^2$ by 2 units to the right (if $f(x) = x^2$, then $(x - 2)^2 = f(x - 2)$). Take a number of points on $y = x^2$, and move them 2 units rightwards. Join the points to give the graph of $y = (x - 2)^2$.

(b) $y = -x^2$ is the reflection of $y = x^2$ in the x-axis. (If $f(x) = x^2$, then $-x^2 = -f(x)$.) Take a few points on $y = x^2$, reflect them in the x-axis, then connect them up to give $y = -x^2$.

Question

The graph of $y = \cos x$ is drawn below. On the same grid, draw the graph of $y = 2\cos x$.

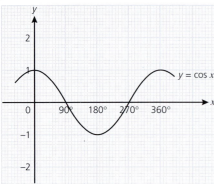

Answer

To find the graph of $y = 2\cos x$ from $y = \cos x$, double the vertical distances of the original graph. (If $f(x) = \cos x$, then $2\cos x = 2f(x)$.)

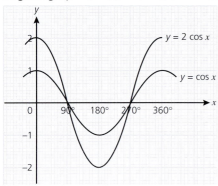

Revision recap

Did you get functions first time?
Questions
The minimum point of $f(x) = x^2$ is at the origin. Write down the coordinates of the minimum point of:
(a) $y = (x + 1)^2$
(b) $y = x^2 - 3$
(c) $y = (x - 2)^2 - 1$
(d) $y = (x + 1)^2 + 4$.

(d) $y = f(x + 1) + 4$; minimum point is $(-1, 4)$.
(c) $y = f(x - 2) - 1$; minimum point is $(2, -1)$
(b) $y = f(x) - 3$; minimum point is $(0, -3)$
(a) This graph is the same as $f(x + 1)$; minimum point is at $(-1, 0)$
Answers

Sine, cosine and tangent graphs

The **sine** and **cosine** graphs look very similar,

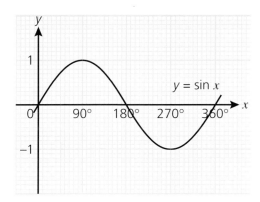

but the sine graph starts at the origin (remember 'original sin')

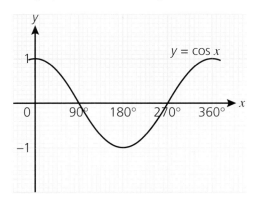

and the cosine graph starts at 1 on the *y*-axis (remember cos1ne).

The graph of **y = tan x** is difficult to draw, but learning it can be avoided by remembering that solutions repeat every 180°.

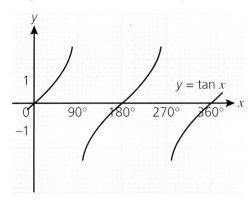

Questions

Solve the following equations for
$0 \leqslant x < 360°$.
(**a**) $\cos x = 0.64$.
(**b**) $\sin x = 0.74$.
(**c**) $\tan x = -0.32$.
(**d**) $\cos x = -0.55$.

Answers

(**a**) The first value can be found from the calculator: $\cos^{-1}(0.64) = 50.2°$.
For the second solution sketch the graphs of $y = \cos x$ and $y = 0.64$: the solutions
are the x-values where the graphs meet.
The second solution is $360 - 50.2 = 309.8°$ (**not** $270° + 50.2°$).
As the first value is $50.2°$ from the peak of the graph, so is the second.
$x = 50.2°, 309.8°$.

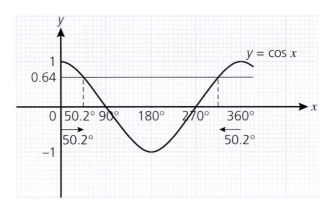

(**b**) From the calculator, $\sin^{-1}(0.74) = 47.7°$.
As the first solution is $47.7°$ from where the graph meets the x-axis, the second is
$47.7°$ back from $180°$ (**not** $90° + 47.7°$).
$x = 47.7°, 132.3°$.

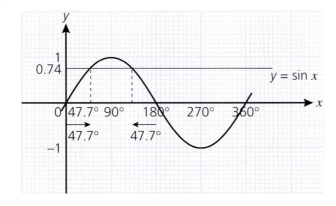

(**c**) $\tan^{-1}(-0.32) = -17.7°$.

Either draw the graph or keep adding 180° to find the two solutions:

$x = 162.3°, 342.3°$.

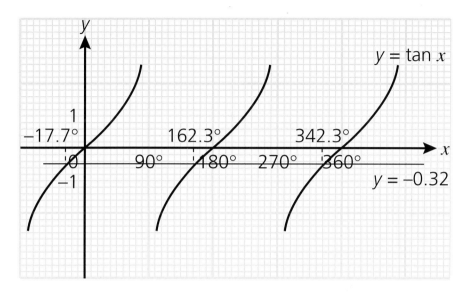

(**d**) From the calculator, $x = \cos^{-1}(-0.55) = 123.4°$.

The other solution is $360° - 123.4° = 236.6°$.

So $x = 123.4°, 236.6°$.

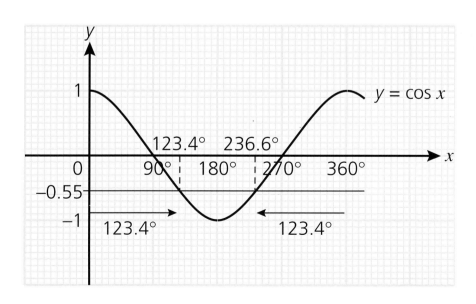

Recognising graphs – Mind Map

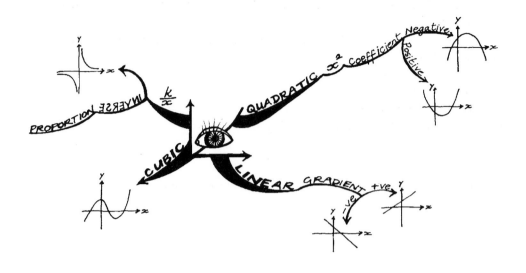

Quiz on solving trigonometric equations
Questions
Solve the equations below for values of x between 0° and 360° inclusive.
(a) $\sin x = 0.72$ (b) $\cos x = 0.56$ (c) $\tan x = 0.35$
(d) $\sin x = -0.45$ (b) $\cos x = -0.18$

Answer

(a) First solution: $x = \text{inv} \sin 0.72 = 46.1°$
Second solution: $x = 180 - 46.1 = 133.9°$
(b) First solution: $x = 55.9°$
Second solution: $x = 360 - 55.9 = 304.1°$
(c) First solution: $x = 19.3°$
Second solution: $x = 19.3 + 180 = 199.3°$
(d) $\text{inv} \sin (-0.45) = -26.7$, but this is outside the given range.
Use graph to help find the other solutions:
$x = 180 + 26.7,\ 360 - 26.7 = 206.7°,\ 333.3°$
(e) First solution: $x = \text{inv} \cos (-0.18) = 100.4°$
Second solution: $x = 360 - 100.4 = 259.6°$

Regions and inequalities

Questions ask to shade – or leave unshaded – the region satisfied by a number of inequalities.

As long as the term in y is positive and on the left-hand side of the inequality, then you may use A⩾OVE, B⩽LOW and BETW⩽⩽N.

So the region indicated by the inequality

$y \leqslant 2x$ is B⩽LOW the line $y = 2x$.

$3x + 4y \geqslant 24$ is the entire region A⩾OVE the line $3x + 4y = 24$.

$0 \leqslant y \leqslant 4$ means the region BETW⩽⩽N $y = 0$ and $y = 4$.

Question

Leave unshaded the region satisfied by the following inequalities:

$$y \leqslant 6 - x$$
$$y \geqslant 1$$
$$x \geqslant 2.$$

Answer

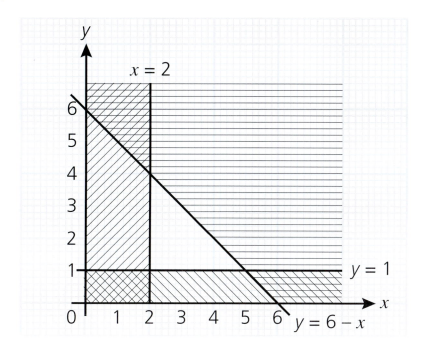

If you are asked to leave the required region unshaded, shade in the side of each graph which is **not** required in the question.

For $y \leqslant 6 - x$, the required region is B⩽LOW the line $y = 6 - x$, so shade the side above the line. Similarly, shade off the region below $y = 1$ and to the left of $x = 2$.

Question

Shade the region satisfied by the following inequalities:

$y \geqslant \frac{1}{2}x$, $5x + 6y \leqslant 30$ and $2 \leqslant x \leqslant 3$.

Answer

Draw on a grid the lines $y = \frac{1}{2}x$, $5x + 6y = 30$, $x = 2$ and $x = 3$.

$y \geqslant \frac{1}{2}x$ is A$\geqslant$OVE $y = \frac{1}{2}x$.

$5x + 6y \leqslant 30$ is B$\leqslant$LOW $5x + 6y = 30$.

$2 \leqslant x \leqslant 3$ is BETW$\leqslant\leqslant$N $x = 2$ and $x = 3$.

Arrows have been drawn on the graphs to show which side of each line the required region lies.

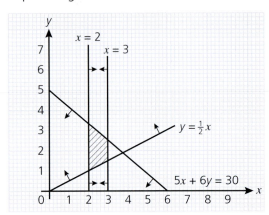

Inequalities and regions

Question

A small tin holds 120 cm³ of sweets and costs £8.00. A large tin holds 360 cm³ and costs £12.00. A newsagent needs to store more than 1200 cm³ of sweets, but has a maximum of £500 to spend on storage containers. Let x be the number of small and y be the number of large tins. Set up two inequalities to represent this information.

Answer

(i) Setting up an inequality for volume:

x small tins holds $120x$ and y large tins hold $360y$

'At least' means 'greater than or equal to'.

$120x + 360y \geqslant 1200$

Dividing through by 120 gives: $x + 3y \geqslant 10$

(ii) Setting up an inequality using the monetary information:

x tins cost $8x$ pounds and y large tins cost $12y$ pounds.

'a maximum of' means 'less than or equal to'.

$8x + 12y \leqslant 500$

Dividing through by 4 gives: $2x + 3y \leqslant 125$

48

Drawing graphs of containers filling

When the cross-section of a container is wide, it will fill slowly; when the cross-section is narrow, it will fill quickly. To draw a graph of a container filling, write down the description of its changing cross-section next to it.
If drawing a container from a graph, write down the description of the rate of increase of the graph at the bottom, middle and top. Relating this to the cross-section should enable you to draw the container.

Questions

Water is poured into vases at a constant rate. Sketch the graph of the depth of water against time for the vases shown.

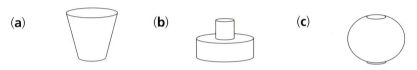

(a)   (b)   (c)

Answers

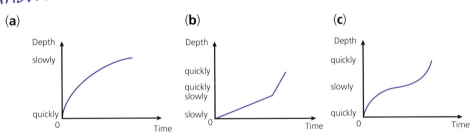

(a)   (b)   (c)

Questions

Water is poured into two vases at a constant rate. The graphs for the depth of water against time are shown below:

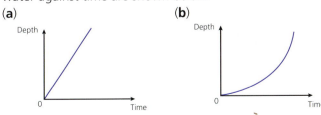

(a)   (b)

Sketch the objects that could be represented by these graphs.

Answers

(a)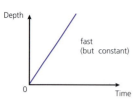

(b)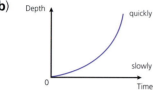

Revision recap

Factorisation: Pick 'n' Mix
Questions

Factorise the expressions below:

(a) $x^2 - 18x + 32$ (b) $12x^2 - 4x$ (c) $6x^2 - 19x + 10$

(d) $x^3 - 4x$ (e) $x^2 - 15x - 54$ (f) $pq - 3p - 2q^2 + 6q$

Answers

(a) $(x - 16)(x - 2)$

(b) $4x(3x - 1)$

(c) $6x^2 - 4x - 15x + 10 = 2x(3x - 2) - 5(3x - 2) = (3x - 2)(2x - 5)$

(d) $x(x - 2)(x + 2)$

(e) $(x - 18)(x + 3)$

(f) $p(q - 3) - 2q(q - 3) = (q - 3)(p - 2q)$

Can you still tackle sequences?
Questions

Find the nth term of the sequences below:

(1) 9, 16, 23, 30, ...   (2) 15, 12, 9, 6, ...   (3) $\dfrac{2}{3}, \dfrac{3}{5}, \dfrac{4}{7}, \dfrac{5}{9}, ...$

(4) 3, 8, 15, 24, ...   (5) 7, 19, 35, 55, ...   (6) 10, 50, 250, 1250, ...

Answers

(1) $7n + 2$

(2) $-3n + 18$

(3) $\dfrac{n + 1}{2n + 1}$

(4) $n^2 + 2n$

(5) $2n^2 + 6n - 1$

(6) 2×5^n

50

Converting curved graphs to straight line graphs

Straight line graphs may be written in the form $y = mx + c$.
Compare the formula in the question with this formula and change the axes accordingly.

Questions

Variables p and t are linked by the formula $p = at^2 + b$.
The following results were obtained during an experiment:

t	0.8	1.2	1.4	1.7	2.2
p	1.9	2.1	2.3	2.6	3.2

By drawing a suitable linear graph, find estimates of the values of a and b.

Answers

Comparing $p = at^2 + b$ with $y = mx + c$: $y = p$, $x = t^2$, $m = a$, and $c = b$.
Add to the table a new row for t^2:

t^2	0.64	1.44	1.96	2.89	4.84

So given the formula $p = at^2 + b$, a linear graph would be obtained by making the horizontal axis t^2 and the vertical axis p.

From the graph below, gradient $= m = a = 0.3$
y-intercept $= c = b = 1.7$.

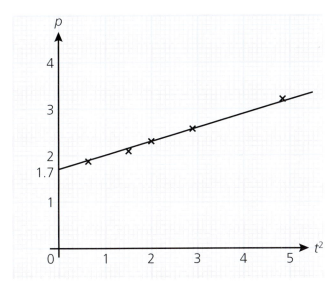

If you are given a table of values of p against t, and asked to find the constants a and b given the equation:

- $p = a\sqrt{t} + b$, you would draw p against $\sqrt{t}$;
  a = gradient and b = value of the y-intercept

- $p^2 = at + b$, make the vertical axis p^2 and the horizontal axis t;
  a = gradient, b = y-intercept.

- $p = at^3 + b$; graph p against t^3;
  gradient = a, y-intercept = b

- $p^3 = at + b$; make the vertical axis p^3 and the horizontal axis t;
  gradient = a, y-intercept = b

- $p = at^2 + bt$; divide through by t to give $\dfrac{p}{t} = at + b$;
  Graph $\dfrac{p}{t}$ against t; gradient = a, y-intercept = b

Graphs and indices

Question

The graph of $y = pq^x$ passes through the points (0,4), (1,6) and (2,k). Find the values of the constants p, q and k.

Answer

Substituting (0,4) gives $p = 4$ because $q^0 = 1$
Substituting (1,6) gives $6 = pq$
$6 = 4q$
$q = 1.5$
Substituting (2,k) gives $k = 4 \times 1.5^2$
$k = 9$.

Length, area and volume   4

Just a few days to go? Top of the list to revise in this section are: Sine and cosine rules; Dimensions.

Scale factors of length, area and volume

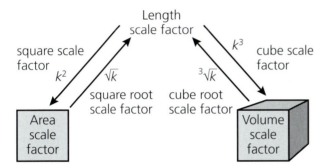

Questions

(**1**) Two similar beer barrels have heights of 0.8 m and 1.2 m.
(**a**) If the smaller barrel has a volume of 0.22 m^3, what is the volume of the larger barrel?
(**b**) If the larger barrel uses 3.1 m^2 of sheet metal, how much sheet metal does the smaller barrel use?

(**2**) Two similar cuboids have surface areas of 420 cm^2 and 650 cm^2. If the smaller cuboid has a height of 9 cm, what is the height of the larger?

(**3**) Two similar objects have volumes in the ratio 8:125. What is the ratio of
(**a**) their heights? (**b**) their surface areas?

(**4**) Two similar tetrahedrons have volumes of 321 cm^3 and 843 cm^3. If the larger tetrahedron has a surface area of 220 cm^2, what is the surface area of the smaller?

Answers

(1)(a) Length scale factor = $1.2 \div 0.8 = 1.5$.

Volume scale factor = $1.5^3 = 3.375$.

Volume of larger barrel = $3.375 \times 0.22 = 0.74 \text{ m}^3$.

(b) Area scale factor = $1.5^2 = 2.25$.

Area of smaller shape = $3.1 \div 2.25 = 1.38 \text{ m}^2$,

or Area scale factor = $(0.8 \div 1.2)^2 = 0.444$.

Area = $0.444 \times 3.1 = 1.38 \text{ m}^2$.

(2) Area scale factor = $650 \div 420 = 1.548$.

Length scale factor = $\sqrt{1.548} = 1.244$.

Height of larger cuboid = $1.244 \times 9 = 11.20 \text{ cm}$.

(3)(a) Ratio of lengths = $\sqrt[3]{8} : \sqrt[3]{125} = 2 : 5$.

(b) Ratio of areas = $2^2 : 5^2 = 4 : 25$.

(4) Volume scale factor = $843 \div 321 = 2.626$.

Length scale factor = $\sqrt[3]{2.626} = 1.380$.

Area of smaller tetrahedron = $220 \div 1.380^2 = 116 \text{ cm}^2$,

or Volume scale factor = $321 \div 843 = 0.381$.

Length scale factor = $\sqrt[3]{0.381} = 0.725$.

Area of smaller tetrahedron = $0.725^2 \times 220 = 116 \text{ cm}^2$.

Always write intermediate values to a generous number of decimal places, or better still, use the memory of your calculator. However, there is no need to write down all the digits on the screen of your calculator. Only round to the requested number of decimal places or significant figures at the end of your working.

Volume of cones and spheres

Volume of a cone of base radius r and height $h = \dfrac{1}{3}\pi r^2 h$.

Volume of a sphere of radius $r = \dfrac{4}{3}\pi r^3$.

Surface area of a sphere of radius $r = 4\pi r^2$.

Question

A toy is made from a hollow hemisphere and cone, as shown. Find the volume of the object.

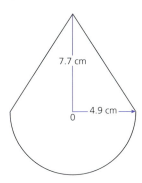

7.7 cm

4.9 cm

0

Answer

Volume of hemisphere $= \dfrac{4}{3}\pi(4.9)^3 \div 2$

$\qquad\qquad\qquad\qquad = 246.4 \text{ cm}^3$.

Volume of cone $\; = \dfrac{1}{3}\pi(4.9)^2(7.7)$

$\qquad\qquad\qquad = 193.6 \text{ cm}^3$.

Total volume $= 440 \text{ cm}^3$.

Question

The toy stands on its hemispherical base, with the cone vertical.
Sand fills the toy to a horizontal level 6.1 cm from the bottom of the toy.
Find the volume of sand used.

Answer

The sand fills the cone up to 1.2 cm from the base.

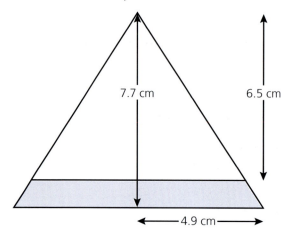

The height of the unfilled cone = 6.5 cm.

Using similar triangles the radius of the unfilled volume is

$4.9 \div 7.7 \times 6.5 = 4.1364$ cm.

Unfilled volume of cone $= \dfrac{1}{3}\pi(4.1364)^2(6.5)$

$= 116.5$ cm³.

Volume of sand $= 246.4 + 193.6 - 116.5$

$= 323.5$ cm³.

Question

A spherical ball has a volume of 10.5 cm³. What is its surface area? Give your answer to 1 decimal place.

Answer

Volume $= \dfrac{4}{3}\pi r^3 = 10.5$

$4\pi r^3 = 31.5$

$r^3 = 2.507$

$r = 1.358$ cm

Surface area $= 4\pi r^2 = 23.2$ cm².

Did you remember to write your answer to 1 decimal place?

Three-dimensional trigonometry

Question

A box is in the shape of a cuboid, of width 28 cm, depth 14 cm and height 11 cm. What is the longest pencil that would fit in the box?

Answer

The longest pencil is the hypotenuse of the shaded triangle.

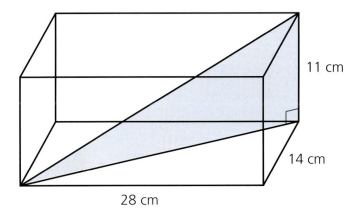

11 cm

14 cm

28 cm

Longest diagonal on the base = $\sqrt{28^2 + 14^2}$
= 31.30 cm.

Longest possible pencil = $\sqrt{31.30^2 + 11^2}$
= 33.2 cm.

Questions

A square-based pyramid has a base length of 5.6 cm and a vertical height of 6.7 cm. Find:
(**a**) the angle between a triangular face and the square base
(**b**) the angle between an edge and the square base
(**c**) the length of an edge from the top of the pyramid to a base vertex.

Answers

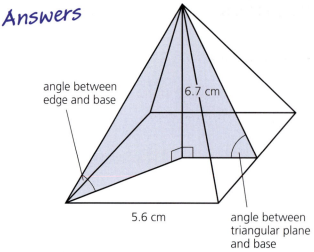

angle between edge and base

6.7 cm

angle between triangular plane and base

5.6 cm

(a) $\tan^{-1}(6.7 \div 2.8) = 67°$

(b) Diagonal of square base $= \sqrt{5.6^2 + 5.6^2}$
$$= 7.92 \text{ cm}$$

Half of diagonal $= 3.96$ cm

Angle $= \tan^{-1}(6.7 \div 3.96) = 59°$

(c) $\sqrt{6.7^2 + 3.96^2} = 7.8$ cm.

Revision recap

Are you sorted with solving equations graphically?
Questions
If the graph of $y = x^2 - 2x$ is given to you, what graph would you draw on the grid to find the solution to (a) $x^2 - 2x = 4$ \qquad (b) $x^2 - 4x - 3 = 0$

Answers

(a) As the left-hand side of the equation is the same as the equation of the graph, draw the graph of $y =$ 'the other side',
$$y = 4$$

(b) You need to get $x^2 - 2x$ on one side of this equation. Since the x^2 is on the left-hand side of the equation, make this side into $x^2 - 2x$ by adding or subtracting terms to both sides:

$$x^2 - 4x - 3 = 0$$
$$+2x + 3 \qquad +2x + 3$$
$$\overline{x^2 - 2x} = 2x + 3$$

So $y = 2x + 3$ should be drawn on the grid.

The solutions to parts (a) and (b) are the x values of the points where the graphs meet.

Sine and cosine rules

When to use the sine or cosine rule

Remember **SALSA CLASS**:
The **S**ine rule links an **A**ngle, **L**ength, **S**ide and an **A**ngle.
The **C**osine rule links a **L**ength, **A**ngle, **S**ide and another **S**ide.

Sine rule

To find a length:
$$\frac{a}{\sin A} = \frac{b}{\sin B} = \frac{c}{\sin C}$$

To find an angle:
$$\frac{\sin A}{a} = \frac{\sin B}{b} = \frac{\sin C}{c}$$

Cosine rule

To find a length: $a^2 = b^2 + c^2 - 2bc \cos A$.

To find an angle: $\cos A = \dfrac{b^2 + c^2 - a^2}{2bc}$.

Questions

Find the lengths or angles marked x in the following triangles:

(a)

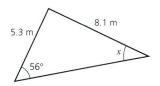

(b)

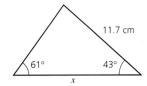

Diagrams not to scale

(c)

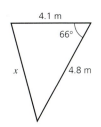

(d)

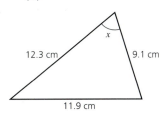

Answers

(**a**) $\dfrac{\sin x}{5.3} = \dfrac{\sin 56°}{8.1} \Rightarrow \sin x = 0.542 \Rightarrow x = 33°.$

(**b**) The angle opposite the side x is $180 - (61 + 43) = 76°$.

$$\dfrac{x}{\sin 76} = \dfrac{11.7}{\sin 61} \Rightarrow x = \dfrac{11.7}{\sin 61} \times \sin 76° \Rightarrow x = 13.0 \text{ cm}.$$

(**c**) It does not matter whether $b = 4.1$ and $c = 4.8$ or $b = 4.8$ and $c = 4.1$.

$$x^2 = 4.1^2 + 4.8^2 - 2 \times 4.1 \times 4.8 \times \cos 66°$$

$$\Rightarrow x^2 = 23.84 \Rightarrow x = 4.9 \text{ m}.$$

(**d**) It is important to label the side opposite the angle as a, or 11.9. Then b and c are 12.3 and 9.1, but it does not matter which way round these are substituted.

$$\cos x = \dfrac{12.3^2 + 9.1^2 - 11.9^2}{2 \times 12.3 \times 9.1}$$

$$\Rightarrow x = \text{inv } \cos(0.413) = 66°.$$

Revision recap

Time to brush up on simultaneous equations from practical situations
Questions
A gardener makes a trellis from a strip of wood. The trellis has 6 horizontal bars, each of length x metres and 3 vertical bars, each of length y metres. It is constructed using 33 m of wood and covers an area of 15 m^2.

(a) Set up two equations in terms of x and y
(b) Show that $2x^2 - 11x + 15 = 0$
(c) Find the possible widths of the trellis.

Answer
(a) Set up one equation for the lengths: $6x + 3y = 33$
and one for the area: $xy = 15$
(b) Rearrange the linear to find y in terms of x: $3y = 33 - 6x$
$y = 11 - 2x$
Then substitute this into $xy = 15$: $x(11 - 2x) = 15$
Expanding and rearranging gives $2x^2 - 11x + 15 = 0$
(c) $(2x - 5)(x - 3) = 0$
$x = 2.5, \ x = 3.$

Remember: if you cannot do parts (a) and (b) in the exam, you should be able to pick up marks on part (c).

Dimensions

Method

(1) Cross out all the numbers (including fractions and π). Do not cross out powers.

(2) Change all of the variables into cm, so x would become cm, c^2 would become cm^2, etc.

(3)(a) Combine the terms where possible: adding like with like makes like.

So cm + cm $\Rightarrow$ cm; cm^2 + cm^2 $\Rightarrow$ cm^2.

(b) Use TIP and DIM where possible.

(c) Write 'none of these' if you've either the sum of terms representing different dimensions such as cm^2 + cm, or a power greater than three.

Questions

In the formulae below the letters a, b, c and d are lengths. Decide whether each expression could be a formula for length, area, volume or none of these.

(i) $\frac{1}{4}\,\pi a(b+c)$

(ii) $\dfrac{3b^2 c}{\pi d}$

(iii) $\sqrt{c^2 + d^2}$

(iv) $3a + b^2$

(v) $\pi abc + 4bd^2$.

Answers

(i) $\frac{1}{4}\,\pi a(b + c) \Rightarrow$ cm(cm + cm) $\Rightarrow$ cm^2, an area.

(ii) $\dfrac{3b^2 c}{\pi d} \Rightarrow \dfrac{\text{cm}^2 \times \text{cm}}{\text{cm}} \Rightarrow \dfrac{\text{cm}^3}{\text{cm}} \Rightarrow$ cm^2, an area.

(iii) $\sqrt{c^2 + d^2} \Rightarrow \sqrt{\text{cm}^2} =$ cm, a length.

(iv) $3a + b^2 \Rightarrow$ cm + cm^2, or 'none of these'.

(v) $\pi abc + 4bd^2 \Rightarrow$ cm $\times$ cm $\times$ cm + cm $\times$ cm^2 $\Rightarrow$ cm^3, a volume.

Congruency

There are four rules for congruency of triangles. The following must be equal in the two triangles:

SSS (side, side, side).

SAS (side, angle and side): the angle must be between the two given sides.

AAS (angle, angle and corresponding side): the given side must be opposite the same angle in both triangles.

HRS (hypotenuse, right angle, side).

Questions

Are the following triangles congruent? If so, give a reason for your answer.

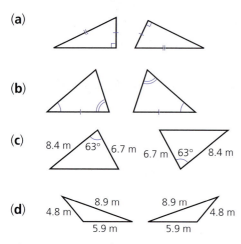

(a)

(b)

(c) 8.4 m 63° 6.7 m 6.7 m 63° 8.4 m

(d) 4.8 m 8.9 m 8.9 m 4.8 m
    5.9 m 5.9 m

Diagrams not to scale

Answers

(**a**) Yes, HRS

(**b**) No – the given side is not opposite the same angle in the two triangles

(**c**) Yes, SAS

(**d**) Yes, SSS.

Going around in circles? The most vital topics in this section are: Circle theorems; Arcs, sectors and segments; Vectors.

Circle theorems

There are seven rules to be learned. These can be classified into three different sections: cyclic quadrilaterals, angles and tangents. Questions often ask for the reason for your answer, so the description for each rule should be memorised.

ACT on circles: Angles, Cyclic quadrilaterals, Tangents

Angles: three rules

The angle subtended by the diameter of a circle is 90°.

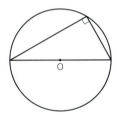

The angle subtended from common points at the centre of a circle is twice the angle at the circumference.

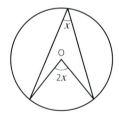 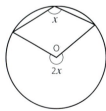

The angles subtended at the circumference from two points are equal.

Cyclic quadrilaterals: one rule

Opposite angles of cyclic quadrilaterals sum to 180°. (Conversely if opposite angles of a quadrilateral sum to 180°, the quadrilateral is cyclic.)

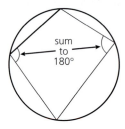

Tangents: three rules

The angle between a tangent and its radius is 90°.

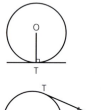

Tangents from a common point are equal.

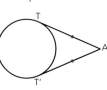

The alternate segment theorem.

Look out for isosceles triangles – those having two radii of the circle for sides are difficult to spot.

Fill in any angles that you find on the diagram, even if the question doesn't ask for them. They may help you find the angles the question does ask for. Always use a pencil when labelling angles on your diagram, just in case you make a mistake.

Questions

The line POR is a diameter of the circle, centre O.
Giving a reason for your answer, find the size of the following angles:

(**a**) QPR (**b**) QSR (**c**) SOR (**d**) ORS

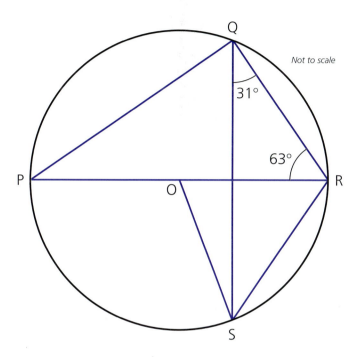

Not to scale

Answers

(**a**) 27°. The angle PQR is 90° because line POR is the diameter.

(**b**) 27°. It is the same as angle QPR because they are subtended from common points.

(**c**) 62°. The angle at the centre is twice the angle at the circumference (SQR).

(**d**) 59°. Triangle ORS is isosceles, because OR and OS are radii.

Questions

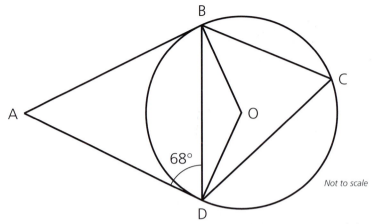

Not to scale

The lines AB and AD are tangents to the circle, centre O. Find the size of the following angles, giving reasons for your answer:

(a) BAD (b) BDO (c) BOD (d) BCD

Answers

(a) 44°
The triangle is isosceles because tangents from a common point are equal.

(b) 22°
The angle between tangent and its radius is 90°.

(c) 136°
Triangle BOD is isosceles (OB and OD are radii).

(d) 68°
Either because it is half the angle at the origin (136°) or it is the same as angle ADB because of the alternate segment theorem.

Arcs, sectors and segments

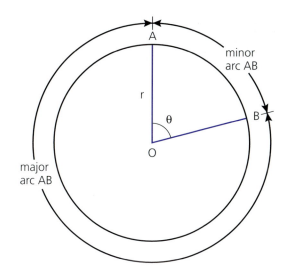

Length of arc $= \dfrac{\theta}{360} \times 2\pi r$

or $\dfrac{\theta}{360} \times \pi d.$

Area of sector $= \dfrac{\theta}{360} \times \pi r^2.$

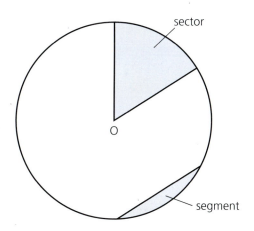

Area of any triangle ABC = $\frac{1}{2}$ ab sin C.

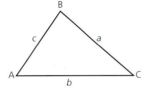

Area of segment = area of sector − area of triangle

Questions

The diagram below shows a circle with the centre O, and radius 16.2 cm.

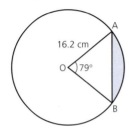

Find:
(**a**) the length of the minor arc AB
(**b**) the area of the sector OAB
(**c**) the area of the shaded segment.

Answers

(**a**) Length of arc = $\dfrac{79}{360}$ × 2π(16.2)

$= 22.3$ cm

(**b**) Area of sector = $\dfrac{79}{360}$ × π(16.2)^2

$= 180.9$ cm^2

(**c**) Area of triangle OAB

$= \frac{1}{2}$ × 16.2 × 16.2 × sin 79

$= 128.8$ cm^2

Area of segment = 180.9 − 128.8
$= 52.1$ cm^2.

Loci and constructions

Locus of points a fixed distance
(**i**) from a point is a circle;
(**ii**) from a line is another line;
(**iii**) from a rectangle is similar to a rectangle, *but with rounded corners.*

Perpendicular bisector

This is a line that is at right angles to a given line and cuts it in two equal parts. Any point on the perpendicular bisector is equidistant from the end points of the given line.

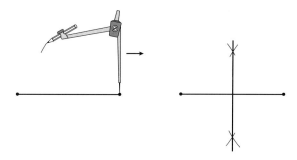

The shortest distance from a point to a line, or the perpendicular from a line to a point.

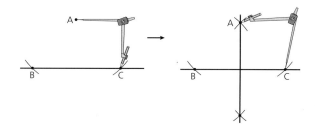

Bisecting an angle

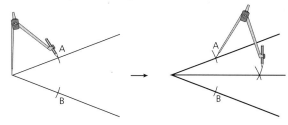

Constructing an angle of 60° or drawing an equilateral triangle

Draw a line. Set your compass to the length of the line, draw arcs from either end of the line. Connect the ends of the line with the points where the arcs cross.

Constructing other angles

To construct angles of 45° and 30°, bisect the angles of 90° and 60° respectively.

Revision recap

Have you got to grips with simultaneous equations from practical situations?

Questions

A runner takes part in a 26 mile race. For the first 16 miles she runs at v mph and for the final 10 miles she slows by 1 mile per hour.

(a) Write an expression for the total time taken in terms of v.
(b) If she runs the race in 4 hours, show that $2v^2 - 15v + 8 = 0$
(c) Hence find her speed.

Answers

(a) For the first 16 miles she takes $\dfrac{16}{v}$ hours

For the final 10 miles she takes $\dfrac{10}{v-1}$ hours

Total time taken $= \dfrac{16}{v} + \dfrac{10}{v-1}$

(b) Substitute time = 4 into your answer from (a) and multiply through by $v(v-1)$:

$4v(v-1) = 16(v-1) + 10v$

$4v^2 - 4v = 16v - 16 + 10v$

$4v^2 - 30v + 16 = 0$

$2v^2 - 15v + 8 = 0$, by dividing through by 2

(c) Use the quadratic formula to solve the equation:

$v = \dfrac{15 \pm \sqrt{(-15)^2 - 4(2)(8)}}{2(2)}$

$v = \dfrac{15 \pm \sqrt{161}}{4} = 6.9, 0.6$

The solution is $v = 6.9$ (if $v = 0.6$, then $v - 1$ is negative).

Remember that even if you cannot get part (b) you can always use the given quadratic equation to find the answer to part (c).

Transformations

Below are the four types of transformations you need to know, and the information which fully describes them:

Reflections 1: line of reflection.
Rotations 3: centre, direction, angle of rotation.
Translations 1: vector.
Enlargements 2: centre, scale factor.

Reflections

Any point on an object, when reflected in a line, ends up equidistant from the line; and the line joining the points is perpendicular to the line of reflection.

Rotations

Most rotations will be of 180° (in which case you do not need to state the direction of the rotation) or 90°.

If you need to find the centre of rotation of an object and its image, connect a point on the object with its point on the image. Draw the perpendicular bisector of this line. Repeat for another pair of points. The centre of rotation is the point where the two perpendicular bisectors meet.

Translations

A translation of $\begin{pmatrix} 2 \\ -5 \end{pmatrix}$ moves the object +2 in the x-direction and −5 in the y-direction.

Enlargements

To find the centre of an enlargement, connect related points on the object and image and then extend them. The centre of enlargement is the point where these lines cross. An enlargement makes the object smaller when the scale factor is between −1 and 1! A negative scale factor means the image is on the opposite side of the centre of enlargement. To find the scale factor of an enlargement, take any length on the image and divide by the related length on the original object.

In the diagram below, the image of P after an enlargement of scale factor $\frac{1}{2}$, centre 0, is Q and the image of P after enlargement of scale factor $-\frac{1}{2}$, centre 0, is R.

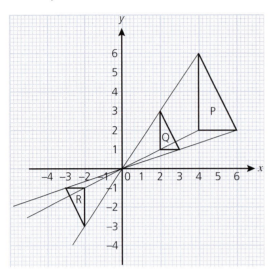

Revision recap

Another look at solving equations graphically
Questions
The graph of $y = x^3 + x^2 - 2x - 5$ is given. Find the equation of the graph you would add to the grid in order to solve:

(a) $x^3 + x^2 - 2x - 3 = 0$
(b) $x^3 + x^2 - 3x - 7 = 0$.

Answers

(a) Make the left-hand side into $x^3 + x^2 - 2x - 5$ by subtracting 2 from both sides:

$$x^3 + x^2 - 2x - 3 = 0$$
$$-2 \quad -2$$
$$x^3 + x^2 - 2x - 5 = -2$$

Therefore $y = -2$ should be drawn on the grid to solve the given equation.

(b) $x^3 + x^2 - 3x - 7 = 0$
$$+ x + 2 \quad + x + 2$$
$$x^3 + x^2 - 2x - 5 = x + 2$$

So draw the graph of $y = x + 2$
The solutions to the equations are the x-values of the points where the graphs meet.

Vector geometry

Vectors have two characteristics: **direction** and **magnitude** (length).

If $\overrightarrow{OA} = \mathbf{a}$, then $\overrightarrow{AO} = -\mathbf{a}$.

Two vectors are parallel (or colinear if they share a common point) if one is a multiple of the other.

Questions

In the diagram $\overrightarrow{OA} = \mathbf{a}$ and $\overrightarrow{OB} = \mathbf{b}$. OACB is a parallelogram. B is the midpoint of $\overrightarrow{CD}$, and E is the midpoint of $\overrightarrow{OB}$.

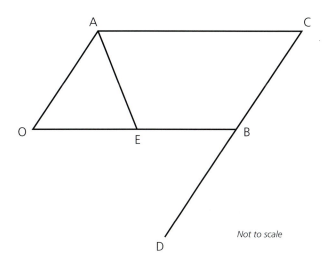

Not to scale

Find, in terms of **a** and **b**, the vectors:

(**a**) $\overrightarrow{OC}$

(**b**) $\overrightarrow{AE}$

(**c**) $\overrightarrow{AD}$

(**d**) Are points A, E and D colinear? Give a reason for your answer.

Answers

(**a**) $\mathbf{a} + \mathbf{b}$.

(**b**) $-\mathbf{a} + \frac{1}{2}\mathbf{b}$ or $\frac{1}{2}\mathbf{b} - \mathbf{a}$.

(**c**) $-2\mathbf{a} + \mathbf{b}$ or $\mathbf{b} - 2\mathbf{a}$.

(**d**) Yes, they are colinear (i.e. they lie in a straight line) because $\overrightarrow{AD}$ is a multiple of $\overrightarrow{AE}$.

73

Questions

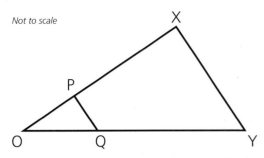

Not to scale

In the diagram $\overrightarrow{OP} = \mathbf{p}$ and $\overrightarrow{OQ} = \mathbf{q}$.

OP:PX = 1:2, and OQ:QY = 1:2. A and B lie on $\overrightarrow{PQ}$ and $\overrightarrow{XY}$ respectively, such that $\overrightarrow{PA} = \frac{1}{4}\overrightarrow{PQ}$ and $\overrightarrow{XB} = \frac{1}{4}\overrightarrow{XY}$.

(a) In terms of **p** and **q**, find the vectors:

    (i) $\overrightarrow{PQ}$

    (ii) $\overrightarrow{OX}$

    (iii) $\overrightarrow{XY}$

    (iv) $\overrightarrow{OA}$

    (v) $\overrightarrow{OB}$.

(b) Write down two comparisons between $\overrightarrow{PQ}$ and $\overrightarrow{XY}$.

Answers

(a) (i) $\mathbf{q} - \mathbf{p}$

    (ii) $3\mathbf{p}$

    (iii) $3\mathbf{q} - 3\mathbf{p}$

    (iv) As $\overrightarrow{PQ} = \mathbf{q} - \mathbf{p}$, $\overrightarrow{PA} = \frac{1}{4}(\mathbf{q} - \mathbf{p})$,

$$\overrightarrow{OA} = \mathbf{p} + \frac{1}{4}(\mathbf{q} - \mathbf{p}) = \frac{1}{4}\mathbf{q} + \frac{3}{4}\mathbf{p}$$

    (v) $\overrightarrow{XY} = 3\mathbf{q} - 3\mathbf{p}$, $\overrightarrow{XB} = \frac{3}{4}\mathbf{q} - \frac{3}{4}\mathbf{p}$,

$$\overrightarrow{OB} = 3\mathbf{p} + \frac{3}{4}\mathbf{q} - \frac{3}{4}\mathbf{p} = \frac{3}{4}\mathbf{q} + \frac{9}{4}\mathbf{p}$$

(b) They are parallel because $\overrightarrow{XY}$ is a multiple of $\overrightarrow{PQ}$. $\overrightarrow{XY}$ is three times the length of $\overrightarrow{PQ}$.

Current and motion

In these questions, an object is travelling in air or water with the current affecting its direction of motion.

You need to consider the direction and speed of:

- the object as if there were no current
- the current
- the actual (or resultant) motion of the object.

If two of the above are perpendicular, they can be drawn as the sides of a right-angled triangle, and the distances involved can be drawn on the triangle. In the diagrams below, the resultant direction is the actual direction of travel when the current is included.

Most questions fall into the following two types:

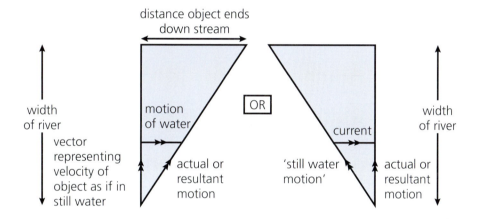

These questions can usually be solved using Pythagoras' theorem, trigonometry or the proportionality of similar figures.

Questions

The current of the river runs parallel to its straight parallel banks at a speed of 0.25 m/s. A boat, travelling at 0.65 m/s crosses the river.

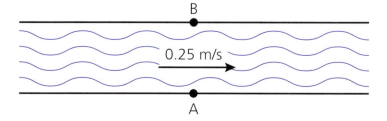

(**a**) (**i**) In which direction must the boat head in order to end up on the other bank at point B, directly opposite point A?

(**ii**) What is its resultant speed?

(**iii**) If the river is of width 60 m, how long will it take to cross?

(**b**) A second boat, travelling at the same speed, crosses from A, constantly facing in a direction perpendicular to the direction of the current.

(**i**) What is its resultant speed?

(**ii**) What is its resultant direction?

(**iii**) How far downstream from B will the boat land on the opposite bank?

(**iv**) How long does it take to cross?

Answers

(**a**)

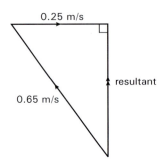

(**i**) $\sin^{-1}(0.25 \div 0.65) = 23°$ from the perpendicular to the bank.

(**ii**) $\sqrt{0.65^2 - 0.25^2}$ = 0.6 m/s.

(**iii**) $60 \div 0.6$ = 100 seconds.

(**b**)

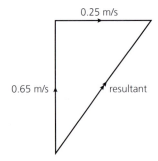

(**i**) $\sqrt{0.65^2 + 0.25^2}$ = 0.70 m/s.

(**ii**) $\tan^{-1}(0.25 \div 0.65) = 21°$ from the perpendicular to the bank.

(iii) It is easiest to use similar triangles here:

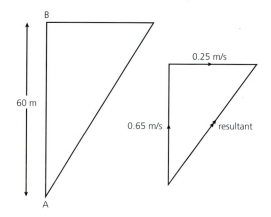

Speed (m/s)　　　　Distance (m)
　0.65　　　　　　　　　60
　0.25

$$\text{Distance} = \frac{0.25 \times 60}{0.65} = 23 \text{ m.}$$

(iv) $60 \div 0.65 = 92$ seconds.

Revision recap

Have a bash at indirect proportion
Questions
y is inversely proportional to x. If $y = 9.4$ when $x = 1.4$, find:
(a) y when $x = 1.7$
(b) x when $y = 10.6$

Answers

$$y \, \alpha \, \frac{1}{x}$$

$$y = \frac{k}{x}$$

$$9.4 = \frac{k}{1.4}$$

$$k = 13.16$$

(a) $y = 13.16 \div 1.7$
$$= 7.7$$

(b) $10.6 = \frac{13.16}{x}$

$$x = 13.16 \div 10.6$$

$$x = 1.24$$

Revision recap

Let's throw some light on dimensions

Questions

The variables a, b, c, and d represent lengths.

Write down next to each of the formulae below whether they are for length, area, volume or none of these.

(i) $\dfrac{3a^2}{2p}$

(ii) $\pi\sqrt{(a^2 - b^2)}$

(iii) $\pi d(a^2 + b^2 + c^2)$

(iv) $4abcd$

(v) $\pi abc + 4b^2$

(vi) $\dfrac{c}{d}(\pi a^2 + 2bc)$

Answers

(i) length
(ii) length
(iii) volume
(iv) none of these
(v) none of these
(vi) area

Do you find linear graphs straightforward?

Questions

(1) Find the gradient and the coordinates of the y-intercept of the graphs below:

    (a) $y = 3x + 2$

    (b) $y = 4 - x$

    (c) $x + 4y = 3$.

(2) Find the equation of the line parallel to $y = 3x + 4$ which passes through the point (2, 1).

Answers

(1) (a) Gradient = 3 y-intercept is (0, 2)

(b) Gradient = −1 y-intercept is (0, 4)

(c) Rearrange to make y the subject of the formula: $y = -0.25x + 0.75$

Gradient = −0.25 y-intercept is (0, 0.75).

(2) If the lines are parallel, they have the same gradient. So the equation of the line is of the form $y = 3x + k$, where k is a constant.

Substitute in (2, 1) to find k: $1 = 6 + k \Rightarrow k = -5$

So the line has equation $y = 3x - 5$.

Statistics and probability 6

From this section, the most probable topics to appear in your exam are: Averages; Standard deviation; Cumulative frequency; Histograms; Probability.

Averages

The **mean** is $\frac{\Sigma x}{n}$ (discrete or non-grouped data) or $\frac{\Sigma fx}{\Sigma f}$ (grouped): remember *fax* over *frequencies*.

Σ (called sigma) means 'the sum of'.

The **median** is the middle value when the data is arranged in order from smallest to largest. The middle value of n items of data is the $\frac{(n+1)}{2}^{th}$ value, but when dealing with cumulative frequency this is usually approximated to the $\frac{n}{2}^{th}$ value.

The **mode** is the most common value.

Questions

Find the (**a**) mean, (**b**) median and (**c**) mode of the following set of data:
3, 5, 7, 6, 8, 6, 5, 8, 8, 4, 3, 5, 6, 5, 5.

Answers

(**a**) Mean $\frac{\Sigma x}{n} = \frac{84}{15} = 5.6$.

(**b**) The median is the $\frac{(15+1)}{2}$ th = 8th value.

The data, when arranged in order, are
3, 3, 4, 5, 5, 5, 5, 5, 6, 6, 6, 7, 8, 8, 8.
So the median is 5.

(**c**) The mode (most common value) is 5.

Averages using grouped data

Questions

A football club played 30 games in a season. The number of goals they scored in the matches are shown below:

No. of goals scored	0	1	2	3	4	5	6	7
Frequency	6	3	4	6	7	2	2	0

Find:

(**a**) the mean,

(**b**) the median,

(**c**) the mode

(**d**) the range of the above data.

Answers

(**a**)

$f \times x$	0	3	8	18	28	10	12	0

$$\text{Mean} = \frac{\Sigma fx}{\Sigma f} = \textit{fax over frequencies} = \frac{79}{30} = 2.63.$$

Note that the total frequency (= $\Sigma f = 30$) is often given in the first line of the question.

(**b**) The median is the $15\frac{1}{2}$ th value.

The first 6 values are 0, the 7th to 9th are 1, the 10th to 13th are 2, the 14th to 19th are 3, etc. Therefore the $15\frac{1}{2}$ th value is 3.

(**c**) Mode = no. of goals with highest frequency = 4.

(**d**) The range = 6 – 0 = 6 (7 has a frequency of zero and so is not the largest value).

Averages using mid-interval values

Questions

Eighty guests attended a party. The distances they drove are shown below:

Distance (x km)	$0 \leqslant x < 5$	$5 \leqslant x < 10$	$10 \leqslant x < 20$	$20 \leqslant x \leqslant 50$
No. of guests	15	26	34	5

Find (i) the mean, (ii) the class in which the median lies and
(iii) the maximum possible range.

Answers

(i)

Mid-interval value	2.5	7.5	15	35
$f \times x$	37.5	195	510	175

$$\text{Mean} = \frac{\Sigma fx}{\Sigma f} = \frac{917.5}{80} = 11.5 \text{ km.}$$

(ii) Median value = $40\frac{1}{2}$ th value, which lies in $5 \leqslant x < 10$.

(iii) Maximum possible range = 50 − 0 = 50.

Revision recap

One more shot at rational and irrational numbers
Questions
(1) (a) Find a rational number between 1.1 and 1.2.
　　(b) Find an irrational number between 17 and 18.
(2) (a) Find a number x other than 3 such that $\sqrt{3} \times \sqrt{x}$ is a rational number.
　　(b) Find a number y such that $\sqrt{3} + y$ is a rational number.

Correlation and the line of best fit

Data on scatter diagrams can be

positively correlated　　　negatively correlated

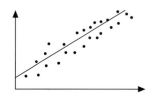 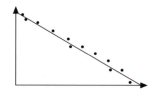

or have **no correlation**.

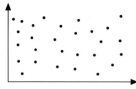

The closer the data lies
to a line the stronger
the correlation.

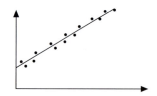

strong positive correlation

The further it is from
the line of best fit, the
weaker the correlation.

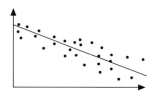

weak negative correlation

Note

When drawing a line of best fit, a good rule of thumb is to ensure that there
are the same number of points either side of the line.

Standard deviation including use of calculators

Entering the data

Discrete data

(1) Set your calculator to SD or STATS mode.
(2) Enter the data, pressing [M+] (DATA) after each item of data.
(3) Check that you have entered the data correctly by checking n, the total frequency.
On SHARP calculators, it is usually shown on the screen when you have pressed [M+] (DATA) after the last value.
On CASIO calculators, it depends on the model you have: either press [SHIFT] [6], or press [Kout][3], or press [RCL][3] or [RCL][3] C

Grouped data

As above, but enter the x value first, then:

* for CASIO calculators, enter either [×] or [SHIFT][;] (depending on the model)
* for SHARP calculators, enter [SHIFT][,] then type in the frequency then press [M+] (Data) or [M+] (DT).

Correcting an entry
Press [SHIFT][CL], [SHIFT][DEL] or [SHIFT][CD] depending upon the type of calculator.

Clearing the statistical memory
Press [SHIFT][Scl], [SHIFT][SAC] or [SHIFT][CA].

Finding:
(1) **the mean**: look above the number keys to find x with a bar above it. Pressing shift then the key gives the mean.
(2) **the standard deviation**: look above the number keys for σ_n (not σ_{n-1}).

Note
If you need to use the formula, you can find Σx^2 and Σx from your calculator.

Understanding the standard deviation

The standard deviation is, like the range and the inter-quartile range, a measure of the spread (or dispersion) of the data.

Adding/subtracting a certain number to every item of data will:

- increase/decrease the mean by this amount
- **not** alter the spread of the data, so it will not affect the standard deviation.

Multiplying each item of data by a constant number will increase both the mean and the standard deviation by the same factor.

Questions

(a) Find the mean and standard deviation of the data below:
5.5, 6.7, 7.1, 7.3, 7.6, 8.8, 9.9, 10.3

(b) If all values were increased by 0.3, what would be the mean and the standard deviation of the data?

Answers

(a) Mean = $\dfrac{\sum x}{n}$ = 7.9

Standard deviation = $\sqrt{\dfrac{\sum x^2}{n} - \left(\dfrac{\sum x}{n}\right)^2}$ or $\sqrt{\dfrac{\sum x^2}{\sum f} - \left(\dfrac{\sum x}{\sum f}\right)^2}$.

$\sum x^2 = 5.5^2 + 6.7^2 + 7.1^2 + 7.3^2 + 7.6^2 + 8.8^2 + 9.9^2 + 10.3^2 = 518.14$

Standard deviation = $\sqrt{\dfrac{518.14}{8} - 7.9^2} = 1.54$.

(b) Mean = 7.9 + 0.3 = 8.2   Standard deviation = 1.54.

Questions

The mean and standard deviation of the data below are 85.5 and 15.1 respectively, to 1 decimal place.
62, 71, 84, 91, 102, 103

(a) Write down in terms of x the mean and standard deviation of:
62 + x, 71 + x, 84 + x, 91 + x, 102 + x, 103 + x

(b) Write down in terms of y the mean and standard deviation of:
62y, 71y, 84y, 91y, 102y, 103y

Answers

(a) Mean = 85.5 + x Standard deviation = 15.1
(b) Mean = 85.5y Standard deviation = 15.1y

84

Histograms

Questions on histograms are best solved by one of two methods: either by counting the number of blocks in each bar; or by using the triplet where **F = frequency**, **FD = frequency density** and **CW = class width**.

Remember

Frank FeeDs CoWs.

Questions

The histogram and table show information about the ages of people attending a zoo on a particular hour.

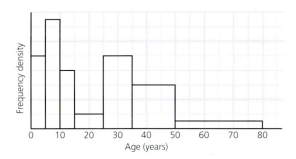

Ages (x years)	Frequency
$0 \leqslant x < 5$	10
$5 \leqslant x < 10$	
$10 \leqslant x < 15$	
$15 \leqslant x < 25$	
$25 \leqslant x < 35$	
$35 \leqslant x < 50$	
$50 \leqslant x < 80$	

(**a**) What is the frequency represented by one square on the grid?
(**b**) Use the histogram to complete the table.

Answers

(**a**) Each square on the grid represents 2 people.
(**b**) The missing values are 15, 8, 4, 20, 18, 6.

Question

One hundred and ten carrots were measured. The results are shown in the table below:

Length (cm)	0–10	–15	–20	–25	–30	–40
No. of carrots	8	10	20	30	26	16

Draw a histogram to illustrate these data.

Answer

Add an extra row for class width:

Class width	10	5	5	5	5	10

From the triplet, $FD = \dfrac{F}{CW}$.

Frequency density	0.8	2	4	6	5.2	1.6

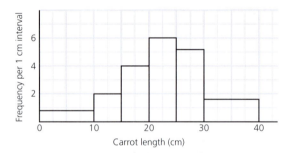

Revision recap

A check up on volumes of cones

Question

A cone is of height 20 cm and radius 5 cm. It is filled with 12 cm of water. The vertex is held downwards, and the circular rim is held horizontally. Find the volume of water in the cone.

Answer

The water in the cone is itself in the shape of the cone, but the radius of this cone is unknown. To find the radius of the cone, use similar triangles.

$$\text{radius} = \frac{12}{20} \times 5 = 3 \text{ cm} \qquad \text{volume of water} = \tfrac{1}{3}\pi r^2 h = \tfrac{1}{3}\pi \times 3^2 \times 12 = 113.1 \text{ cm}^3$$

Cumulative frequency

Remember

When drawing a cumulative frequency graph, plot the graph using the endpoints of the class widths.

The inter-quartile range is the result of subtracting the lower quartile ($\frac{n}{4}$ th value) from the upper quartile ($\frac{3n}{4}$ th value).

On the graph, the frequency is written on the vertical axis.

Questions

A test was given to 72 students. Their marks, out of 70, are summarised in the table below:

Mark	0–10	11–20	21–30	31–40	41–50	51–60	61–70
Frequency	4	8	12	16	22	8	2

(a) Complete the cumulative frequency table.

Mark	0–10	0–20	0–30	0–40	0–50	0–60	0–70
Cumulative frequency	4	12					

(b) Draw a cumulative frequency graph for the data.
(c) From your graph, estimate (i) the median and (ii) the inter-quartile range.
(d) The pass mark was 45 out of 70. From your graph, estimate the percentage of students who passed the test.
(e) The cumulative frequency graph for a second set of students is shown. Make two comparisons between the results of the two groups.

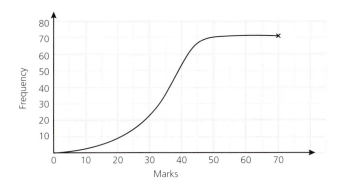

87

Answers

(a) The missing entries are 24, 40, 62, 70, 72.

(b)

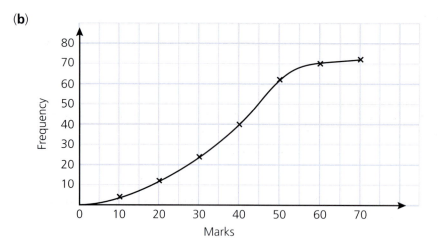

(c) (i) median = 38 approx. (the median value is the 36th).
   (ii) inter-quartile range = upper quartile (54th value) – lower quartile
       (18th value) = 47 – 26 = 21 (approx).

(d) From the graph, 45 marks corresponds to roughly 50 people.
   Therefore about 22 people scored **above** 45 marks. 22 ÷ 72 × 100 = 31%.

(e) The median in the second set of data is lower, the percentage passing is lower.
   (You may compare the inter-quartile range instead.)

Revision recap

A last look at solving simultaneous equations by substitution
Question
Solve $3x - 4y = 37$
          $y = 3 - x$

Answer

Substitute the second equation into the first. Replace y in the first equation
with $(3 - x)$. $3x - 4(3 - x) = 37$
Expand the brackets, remembering to multiply through by -4:
$3x - 12 + 4x = 37$
Simplify: $7x - 12 = 37$
Solve to find x: $7x = 49$ $x = 7$
Substitute in the second equation to find y: $y = 3 - x$ $y = -4$
Check in the first equation: $3 \times 7 - 4 \times -4 = 37$ ✓

88

Surveys and sampling

Surveys

You may be asked to comment on a questionnaire or survey. You should think about the following issues.

(1) The way the question is worded.
(a) Is it a leading or biased question? (i.e. is it trying to push the interviewee into answering in a certain way, such as by using "Don't you think...")
(b) Is it ambiguous? (i.e. could the question be interpreted in more than one way?)

(2) The range of responses.
If the interviewee answers by ticking a box, are all possible answers covered once (also called 'inclusive') and only once?

Remember

ALIB1.
Is the question:
Ambiguous
Leading
Inclusive
Biased
1 and only 1 possible response, if there are boxes to tick?

Sampling

In statistical research, it is almost impossible to collect data from every possible unit that is involved. To save time, effort and money, a sample is taken.

A **random sample** is a sample taken entirely at random! This is in contrast to a **stratified random sample**, where groups are represented in the sample according to their size in the population. For example, if a stratified random sample were to be taken of the entire population of a country of which 15% was over 70 years old, then 15% of the sample would be over 70 years old.

Remember

When tackling questions on surveys, remember the following, or you'll be **SoRRy**:

(1) **S**ize – is the sample big enough?

(2) **R**epresentative – are all types represented?

(3) **R**andomness – is the sample unbiased?

Probability

When you see 'or' in a question, you can usually use **ADORE**: add = or.
For 'and', use times (remember **SAND TIMER**).
When two events are **mutually exclusive**, they cannot occur simultaneously.
When two events are **independent**, the outcome of one does not affect the outcome of the other.

A **table of outcomes** is often used when two dice are thrown. The most common table of outcomes is for the sum of the scores of two dice.

Relative frequency $= \dfrac{\text{number of times event occurs}}{\text{total number of trials}}$.

Expected frequency = number of trials × probability.

Questions

A child rolled a die 90 times and recorded the results.

Score	1	2	3	4	5	6
Frequency	9	17	13	20	18	13

(a) Write down the relative frequency of a score of 5.
(b) If the die were unbiased, what would you expect to be the frequency of a score of 2?

Answers

(a) Relative frequency $= \dfrac{18}{90} = \dfrac{1}{5}$.

(b) If the die were unbiased, the probability of scoring 2 would be $\dfrac{1}{6}$, so the expected frequency $= 90 \times \dfrac{1}{6} = 15$.

Questions

At a fairground, a person is given two darts to throw at a dartboard. For each bull's-eye she hits, she wins a prize. If the probability that she hits the bull's-eye with a dart is 0.3, find the probability that she:
(a) wins 2 prizes
(b) wins exactly one prize.

Answers

(a) $0.3 \times 0.3 = 0.09$
(b) She may hit the bull's-eye with either the first or second dart.
$0.3 \times 0.7 + 0.7 \times 0.3 = 0.42$
(This may be solved using a tree diagram.)

Questions

Two fair dice are thrown. The smaller score is subtracted from the larger score.
(**a**) What is the probability that the difference is zero?
(**b**) What is the probability that the difference is greater than 3?

Answers

Firstly set out a table of outcomes:

		First die					
		1	2	3	4	5	6
	1	0	1	2	3	4	5
	2	1	0	1	2	3	4
Second	3	2	1	0	1	2	3
die	4	3	2	1	0	1	2
	5	4	3	2	1	0	1
	6	5	4	3	2	1	0

(**a**) $\dfrac{6}{36} = \dfrac{1}{6}$. (**b**) $\dfrac{6}{36} = \dfrac{1}{6}$.

Questions

A bag contains three red counters and four green counters. Three counters are chosen at random. Each time a counter is withdrawn it is not replaced. Calculate the probability that:
(**a**) the first two counters chosen are red;
(**b**) the second counter chosen is green;
(**c**) all three counters are of the same colour.

Answers

(**a**) Remember that after the first red counter has been taken there are two red counters out of six.

$$\frac{3}{7} \times \frac{2}{6} = \frac{1}{7}.$$

(**b**) The first counter may be red or green:

$$\frac{3}{7} \times \frac{4}{6} + \frac{4}{7} \times \frac{3}{6} = \frac{4}{7}.$$

(**c**) The counters may be all red or all green:

$$\frac{3}{7} \times \frac{2}{6} \times \frac{1}{5} + \frac{4}{7} \times \frac{3}{6} \times \frac{2}{5} = \frac{1}{7}.$$

Question

In a small village, the probability that a person plays for the bowls team is $\frac{1}{7}$.

The probability that a person wears glasses is $\frac{3}{7}$. Why is the probability of

a person playing for the bowls team or wearing glasses **not** necessarily $\frac{4}{7}$?

Answer

The short answer is because the events may not be mutually exclusive. That is, there may be some people that are both playing for the bowls team and wearing glasses. If the probabilities are added together, these people will be double counted.

Tree diagrams

In tree diagrams, all branches from a common point add up to 1.

Questions

An apple is growing on a tree. The probability of it falling this week is 0.8. If it does not fall this week, the probability that it falls next week is 0.9.
(**a**) Draw a tree diagram to represent this information.
(**b**) (**i**) Calculate the probability that it will fall next week.
   (**ii**) Calculate the probability that the apple will have fallen by the end of next week.

Answer

(**a**)

(**b**) (**i**) Probability that it falls next week is $0.2 \times 0.9 = 0.18$.
   (**ii**) This is the probability that it falls this week or the probability that it falls next week, $0.8 + 0.18 = 0.98$.

Questions

A boy either walks or takes the bus to school. If it is raining, the probability that the boy walks to school is $\frac{1}{6}$. If it is not raining, the probability that he goes by bus is $\frac{1}{2}$.

If the probability of it raining on any particular day is $\frac{1}{4}$:

(**a**) draw a tree diagram to represent this information;
(**b**) find the probability that he walks to school.

Answers

(**a**)

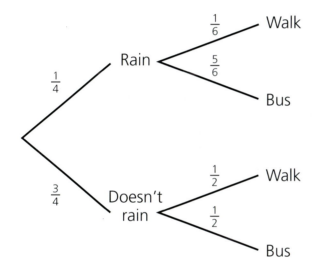

(**b**) Start from the 'root' of the tree diagram – there are two different ways by which he can walk.

Probability that he walks is $\frac{1}{4} \times \frac{1}{6} + \frac{3}{4} \times \frac{1}{2} = \frac{5}{12}$.

Hints and Tips

Before you go into the exam:
- Check your calculator: is it in 'degrees' mode and out of any other mode, such as standard deviation?
- Do you have all the right equipment?
- Do you know the dates and times of all your exams? Check and double check!
- Is your alarm clock working?

When you are in the exam:
- Write legibly.
- Use the memory of your calculator if you are tackling a long question (you must be out of SD or STATS mode to use the memory).
- Make it clear to examiners exactly what you mean, such as the labelling of regions or equations of lines.
- Always leave construction lines on diagrams and graphs: such as compass arcs for perpendicular bisectors and lines showing median and inter-quartile range on cumulative frequency graphs.
- Remember to give units for your answer, such as cm^2, kg or litres if the paper doesn't already do it for you.
- If you can't do a question come back to it later.
- Always show your working.
- If you can't do part (**a**), try to pick up some marks on later parts – there are often hints in the question.
- Check that you have written your answers to the specified number of decimal places or significant figures.

After the first exam:
- Go back to the contents list of the book and cross off the topics that came up on the first paper. Revise thoroughly those that didn't.
- Don't waste time chatting about it with your friends. You have much better things to do, like revising for your next exam.

Good luck!

Number

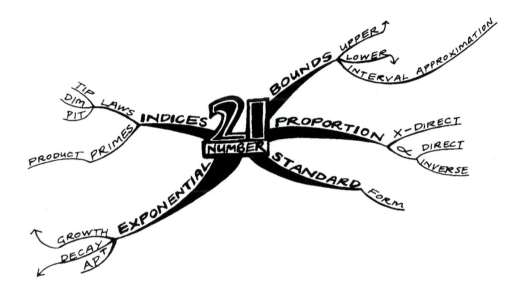

Algebra and graphs

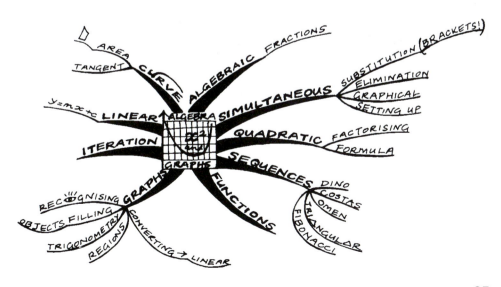

Shape, space and measure

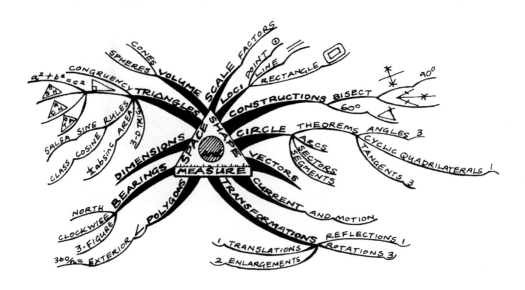

Handling data

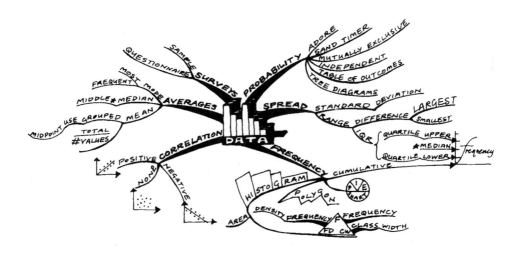